MW00605254

HIDDEN HISTORY

of

ROUTT COUNTY

HIDDEN
HISTORY
of
ROUTT
COUNTY

Rita Herold

THE
History
PRESS

Published by The History Press
Charleston, SC
www.historypress.com

First published 2020

ISBN ˙9781540243805

Library of Congress Control Number: 2020938433

Notice: The information in this book is true and complete to the best of our knowledge. It is offered without guarantee on the part of the author or The History Press. The author and The History Press disclaim all liability in connection with the use of this book.

CONTENTS

PREFACE

Today, the Laughlin Buttes—the tall, dramatic volcanic spires north of Yampa, along Colorado Highway 131, stand as a reminder of the Laughlin family. The Laughlin family came into the valley in the mid-1880s; Tom was two years old, and Ben was ten. When they were older, both of these fellows enjoyed talking to children, and they were articulate tellers of tales. Herb Moore first came into the Yampa area in 1887; he also loved to share his knowledge and to tell stories. I listened to those accounts from the time I was small.

This book is a companion and geographical expansion to my first book, *Yampa Valley's Lost Egeria Park*. During the process of my research and compilation of accounts about the history of Routt County, my extended family and friends graciously shared their stories as well. This work contains not only items from my grandfathers and great-uncles but also a broader scope of Routt County and northwestern Colorado. The Montgomery family arrived in the early 1880s; the Bartz, Nay and Herold families all arrived before 1915. The pioneers of one hundred plus years offer gems of remembered information.

The personnel of the area museums have certainly been generous with their time, archives and photos: Dan Davidson at the Museum of Northwest Colorado in Craig, Laurel Watson with the Hayden Heritage Center, Nita Naugle at the Tracks and Trails Museum in Oak Creek, Wendy Moreau from the Yampa-Egeria Museum and Katy Adams with the Tread of the Pioneers Museum in Steamboat Springs. A thank-you to staff and publishers of The

History Press for their help in this process of getting my works published. Thank you to all who have contributed to this book and thanks to my family for their liberal help, patience and support.

A few of these stories seem far-fetched by today's standards, but the people of that era had to be hardy to survive. May you enjoy these stories that were formerly hidden and tucked away in my files.

OUTLAWS, CRIMINALS
AND OTHER CROOKS

W henever I asked my grandfather Herb Moore or my great-uncle Tom Laughlin to tell stories about the bandits and outlaws that were in the area when it was first settled, they would usually reply that there was not much trouble in the area; it was a peaceable place to live. Perhaps it was the pioneer way of remembering the good times and forgetting the bad, or perhaps some of the incidents that occurred just didn't seem that bad. When I asked specific questions about horse thieves or gunfights, the following incidents came to light. Included is a collection of reports from the early newspapers to give a general idea of what was occurring at the time. A story involving the Bird family was related to me by Tom Laughlin. A similar account, written by Lettie (Mrs. E H.) Godfrey, was printed in the *Steamboat Pilot* many years ago:

> *The story goes that one year a team of horses belonging to him* [William C. Bird] *was stolen from his place in Florissant and for a time no trace of them could be found. Finally, a rumor reached him that the thief had driven the team into Egeria Park. He and his son Albert started at once in pursuit, along with S.D. Wilson of Breckenridge, who was a deputy sheriff.*
>
> *They came upon one of the horses in what is now known as the VanCamp Grove, near the present town of Yampa. Soon, the man who stole them returned, riding the other horse. At first he declined to give up the team but at the sight of the warrant for his arrest he changed his mind.*

That was William Bird's first sight of Egeria Park. The open spaces seemed an opportunity for making a home; he made up his mind to return and bring his family. That incident occurred in 1880.[1]

Ed Watson was at his homestead, just east of the present Yampa cemetery, when the next story took place. Since Watson was involved in this event, the fight would have occurred in the very first years that the homesteaders were in the valley, sometime between 1881 and 1884.

Two horse thieves came through the Egeria Park area. The local residents formed a posse and chased these thieves to an area about ½ mile south of the present town of Yampa. This area was covered by a thick stand of willow trees. This included the larger tree willows, as well as the smaller bushy species of willow. The posse managed to surround the rustlers in this thick stand of trees. The horses were retrieved, but the thieves managed to stay hidden.

As it got dark, one of the posse members heard something rustling in the trees and shot, just missing one of the other members of the posse. The posse decided it was too dangerous to stay in the area where someone might get hurt, so they took all the horses and rode back to Ed Watson's cabin. [If this was the closest habitation to the area of the fight, this would have happened in 1881.] *The guys from the posse put all the horses in the barn and went into the cabin to eat supper. After they had eaten, they sat around talked about the events of the day, and told how close that shot had been. Suddenly, the horse thieves threw open the door and held the entire group at gunpoint.*

The one thief exclaimed, "You may think that we're going to go out of this country on foot, but we're not!"

One of the outlaws kept the group at the table covered, while the other man took Ed Watson to the barn to saddle the horses. When telling about it afterwards, Ed Watson said that he could have jumped the one horse thief while they were saddling the horses, but it might have created a ruckus and notified the other thief still in the house that something was wrong. Ed did not feel that two horses were worth anyone's life. As a result, the thieves left and took the horses with them. There was no pursuit.[2]

Most people who have lived in South Routt County for a while have heard the "Story of the Bird Fight." This story has been handed down and repeated many different times. One time, after I told my version of the story,

The outlaws hid in thick stands of willows where the ground was moist and swampy. *Herold family collection.*

I heard, "That is not the way it happened! There were others in the fight." This led me to collect eleven different versions of the fight when (William) Thomas Bird was killed.

Any oral history is open to interpretation. When one is working with handed-down family histories, this is especially true. Human ego has the storyteller wanting one's own family to be perceived as heroic, thoroughly good, wickedly bad or at least exceptional in some way.

Another thing we need to remember when thinking about the Bird fight is that very little was said about this dispute for twenty years or more. The people involved did not want the authorities (sheriff or marshal) to be involved. Even though the participants felt they were in the right, people were killed. Another aspect was to keep the knowledge of the killings from the thieves' friends or relatives. The Birds did not want anyone trying to "get even."

Something else I found when researching the stories was there were several different men all named Lewis at that time. This could have been a factor in some of the confusion when the story was told. When the name was used, each family immediately thought of its own Lewis.

Lewis Bird would have been nineteen or twenty years old at the time of the fight. There were two Lewis Wilsons. The older Lewis (Lewis L., son of

James Wilson and Betty Ann Bird) came into the area with the first group of settlers. The younger Lewis (son of William Wilson and Rebecca Bowles) came into the valley a year or two later. Mark Choate, another of the early settlers, had a son named Lewis. Finally, Lewis Phillips (son of John Phillips) was born in Yampa area just a few years after the fight. These fellows were all cousins, which adds another detail to the story.

Frances (Bird) Laughlin was a first cousin to Albert, Tom and Lewis Bird. Frances Laughlin came into Routt County with her family in 1885 and they settled about one mile north of the William Bird family.[3] The version of the Bird brothers' Fight that was passed down in her family is slightly different from any of the other versions. Both H.E. Moore and Francis Moore worked with Albert Bird in the slaughterhouse a shy quarter mile south of the Moore family home. The families were close friends, and both the men and the women visited back and forth regularly. The first time I heard the story was from that account.

Because of all these aspects, I don't suppose we will ever know the true story of the Bird fight, but this account is as accurate as I can interpret the story from the many different legends.

The Bird family realized that Egeria Park would be settled quickly, and they wanted to get their choice of homesteads, so the three oldest boys rode into South Routt in the spring of 1881. Albert would have been about twenty-six years old; Tom, twenty-four; and Lewis nineteen or twenty. They worked hard and built the homestead cabin for Albert. This was a small rough cabin that was "cut with axes." They would live in this cabin over the winter as the rest of the Bird family planned on joining them the next summer after finishing their business contracts in Florissant, Colorado.

They had brought several horses (and possibly a mule or two) with them, the ones they had ridden, as well as those used to carry their supplies and equipment. This included such items as axes, scythes, hammers, pans, winter food, etc. Those are all heavy, but those items were needed to carve out a homestead. All of the animals were going to need winter feed. The cutting of meadows was the first step in getting enough hay to winter their horses. They used their scythes in the small openings of the willows to cut the tall wild grasses for the coming winter.

This was a new country, and no one locked their doors; most people didn't even have a lock on their door. Visitors could help themselves to a cup of coffee or get in out of the rain if the weather was bad—that was the cordiality of the land.

The cabin built by the "Bird Boys" in the summer of 1881. The peaked roof was added later; the first roof was rounded in the pioneer way. *Herold family collection, 2006.*

That particular morning, the Bird brothers had gone out into the willows to cut more hay, just as they had been doing for the last several days. The youngest boy, Lewis, left his new boots inside the house and wore some old shoes with gunnysack strips tied around them because he certainly didn't want to go into the wet, boggy ground with his new boots. They would have to last him all winter, as he wouldn't have time or leather to make new ones.

When the Bird "boys" got back to their cabin, they found that someone had come by and stolen all their winter supplies and that pair of new boots. They immediately caught and saddled their horses and followed the tracks. They caught up with the thieves "in the oak hills near Oak Creek Canyon." Shots were exchanged; no one knew for sure who shot who, but when all was over, the two thieves were dead, and Tom Bird was also killed.

The two surviving brothers quickly gathered up their stolen supplies and brought the body of their brother back and buried him near the cabin they had just built.

After losing their brother, Albert and Lewis had no desire to spend the winter in their cabin, so they went back to tell their parents of Tom's death and spent the winter in Florissant. The next summer, the whole family (this included several families of cousins) came back to the Yampa Valley to live.

This stone was placed on Tom Bird's grave twenty-five or more years after Tom was killed. Records indicate that he was killed in 1881. *Herold family collection.*

The important detail in this version of the Bird fight seems to be that the only participants were the outlaws and the Bird brothers.

Information about the Birds includes these facts: Albert Bird took up homestead rights on the place where the Bird brothers' original cabin was built. The original cabin is now part of the shed (shop) just north of the two-story frame house that Albert built several years later. At the time of this writing, both the cabin and the frame house that Albert built are still standing.

The boys' parents (William and Mary Bird) homesteaded just south of the original cabin. William and Mary's place became known as the Do Drop In. William's first cabin was the log building a few yards west of what is now considered the William Bird homestead.

After looking at the different versions of this Bird fight and researching the available manuscripts and diaries about the various Bird families, I believe that there were three different fights. The first was the fight between the Birds (William and Albert) and the thieves who stole the team. The second fight was the preceding, when Tom Bird was killed. The third fight occurred at the Ed Watson homestead between horse thieves and some of the early homesteaders.

When relating and repeating the different stories, the details and names of people were switched, confused and combined. The only one of these three fights in which anyone was killed was the fight when Tom Bird was shot, making this the most important and dramatic event when retelling the tale.

The exploits of the notorious outlaws Harry Tracy and David Lant have been recorded in many different places. The following is a version of the recapture of Tracy told by Herb Moore. Herb and Bertha Moore were good friends of Charley and Ruby Neiman. Francis Moore, Herb's son, mentioned this was a portrayal that he had neither read nor heard elsewhere.[4]

Sheriff Neiman captured Tracy in Brown's Park and took him to the Hahn's Peak jail. The following story occurs when Tracy knocked Neiman out to escape from that jail. Tracy and Lant stole the stage horses and rode them to a point where they could catch the stagecoach.

After Tracy had overpowered Neiman and escaped toward Steamboat, Neiman followed, but he (Neiman) left his horse and got on the stage as a passenger. They were sure that Tracy would stop at Laramore's house to get on the stage to leave the country, as he had used that means of escape before.

"The Bear Cage" jail cell at Hahn's Peak, Colorado. Notice that it is a cage inside a cage. *Herold family collection, 2006.*

The Laramore house near Sidney, Colorado, was a normal stop for the stagecoach. [Samantha Laramore was the daughter of William and Mary Bird of Yampa.]

The stage driver asked Neiman, "What'll I do?"

Neiman told the driver to go ahead just as he normally would. When the stage stopped in front of Laramore's house, Tracy opened the door to get into the stage. Neiman poked a gun in Tracy's face and told him he was under arrest.

Tracy blurted out, "Why you little devil, I thought I killed you yesterday!"

Since Tracy had already escaped once, Neiman was not going to chance him getting loose again. Neiman used a twenty-foot log chain around Tracy's and Lant's feet and fastened it with padlocks. There was no place in Routt County that would hold Tracy, so Neiman contacted the sheriff from Pitkin County and asked him to come and get Tracy. When that Sheriff arrived and took Tracy a prisoner, Neiman tried to tell him that Tracy was a desperate man and he would escape if there was any possible chance. The Sheriff was a "big-shot" and would not listen to someone from a "backwoods place" like Routt County. Before too long, Tracy and Lant managed to escape from the new jail of Pitkin County.[5]

Shannan Sparkman wrote about the incident on website of the Museum of Northwest Colorado at Craig, adding that Tracy and Lant claimed innocence in Valentine Hoy's murder, but officers were not convinced, and the pair was transported to the Hahn's Peak Jail to await trial.[6]

They had been in jail less than a month when they overpowered Sheriff Neiman, knocked him out and locked him in a cell. They made their escape on two stage horses stolen from a nearby stable and stopped along the route to get saddles. They planned to catch the stage for Wolcott to get out of the territory.

Tracy and Lant were waiting for the stage the next morning at the Laramore Ranch. They had evaded law officers before, and they were sure that they had done it again. The stage pulled up in a swirl of dust, and the two made ready to board. Their plans were quickly changed when they discovered that the passengers already on board included Sheriff Neiman and a deputy. There was nothing to be done but surrender peacefully.

The pair was sent to the jail in Aspen after their recapture.

Lant and Tracy escaped from the Aspen jail and traveled to the West Coast, where a posse shot them.

Ralph Maddox told Francis Moore, "The people that lived down in the Brown's Park area were mighty tough characters." Moore said at the time he just took that statement at face value; it was several years later that he realized Maddox must have been pretty tough, also, or he would not have been able to survive with the "tough ones."

Ralph Maddox told stories of the early days of Brown's Park and of the Basset family.[7] Eb Basset's cabin was even farther up the mountain than Maddox's cabin. Ralph jokingly said that "the farther up the mountain you went, the tougher the people got."

Since they were close neighbors, Ralph and Eb were good friends. They remained friends even when the Bassets were called cattle rustlers and were on the 2 Bar Cattle Company's list of wanted men. That list contained the names of homesteaders whom the 2 Bar accused of rustling cattle. The 2 Bar had a "hired killer" to shoot all the homesteaders on that list.

It was open range, so there were no fences to separate the different ranches. Each rancher drove the neighbor's cattle off the grass that was needed for his own stock. Part of the fight between the various people in Brown's Park was caused by the large cattle ranches having more livestock than there was grass. In turn, the large ranchers accused the smaller ranchers and homesteaders of rustling and butchering other peoples' cattle. Some of the accusations from both sides were undoubtably true.

Ralph Maddox was sitting on a wagonload of logs in Brown's Park about 1925. *Herold family collection.*

> *Ralph told of one incident when he and Eb Basset were slowly drifting about twenty head of 2 Bar cattle up a valley and were almost to the top of a ridge when suddenly Eb stopped and said, "I have a feeling we better leave these cattle right here and not go on." They turned and rode away. Ralph said that it seemed to be a "sixth sense" of Eb's because they learned later that the hired killer and another one or two men were waiting just over that ridge top. They would have opened fire if he and Eb had stuck their heads over the ridge.*[8]

At the time Routt County was first being settled, the criminal element from the settled areas of Colorado would occasionally use the route through Routt County to escape. They would travel down Egeria Park and through Twenty Mile Park to Craig, Lay and on into the Brown's Park area. That gave them the option of going to either Wyoming or Utah to evade the Colorado authorities. At that time, what is now Moffat County was all part of Routt County.

Even though the movies have romanticized or perhaps ridiculed the idea of the outlaws using an actual "Outlaw Trail" during the early days of settlement in the West, the criminal element did have favorite areas to escape capture. The outlaws could travel from the Hole-in-the-Wall in Wyoming and cut through Brown's Park in Colorado to get to Robber's Roost in Utah.

The entire area was relatively uninhabited, and the people who did live and ranch in the area did not report travelers to the authorities. The most famous and most rugged part of that trail was through Brown's Park and across Diamond Mountain to Vernal, Utah.

Avvon Chew Hughel related the following story about the range war in Utah in 1896:

Two of the Chew siblings, Leath [Avvon], age eight, and Harry, age eleven, were alone in their cattle camp and practicing their shooting skills:

A rider came through the gap and into camp before we realized it was not Dad who was riding Tuffy, but Tom Dilley, a cattleman who often brought small surprises to my brothers and myself when we were left on the job. We hailed him, but something in his bearing toned down our usual exuberant greeting.

"Harry," he asked, "where's Dunk?"

"Right there," Harry replied, pointing to the clump of quaking aspen.

"Will you get him quick?" Tom asked, as he began stripping gear from his exhausted horse.

Harry led Dunk, a big rangey sorrel, to Tom's saddle which was promptly strapped on. Then Tom did something that we could not understand. He took Harry's saddle and put it on his own jaded Tuffy. Turning to us, he said, "Now both of you listen closely. Leave Tuffy right where he is and you, Leath, take the thirty-thirty over into the rocks there. Harry, you take the forty-four and go across the ravine and get down in those rocks on the other side of the trail. In a little while a bunch of men, five or six, will come up the trail. You must keep down, keep outa sight. Don't let 'em see you whatever you do. Now, Harry when the first men get to that little black bush..."

"That's a scrub cedar," interrupted Harry.

"When the first men get to that scrub cedar, you put a bullet in the trail in front of them. Don't hit anyone and don't hit a horse either. They will stop, and after talking maybe they will start to come on, and if they do, Leath, you shoot into the trail in front of them. Think you are a good enough shot not to hit anyone? I am sure they won't try to come up through the gap there. Whatever they do you two keep outa sight."

"But, Tom..." I began as he started for Dunk.

"Haven't time, Leath," and he mounted. "Good-bye for now," he said, as Dunk took up the trail and disappeared over the rise in a direction that would take him down Nine Mile toward Brock's Ranch.

Harry and I chose our positions in the rocks. We lay on our bellies with our guns dead rest, pointing down the trail. Seemed I had waited a long time—it could have been twenty minutes., when I saw the dust just before the riders emerged 'round the hill.

"There they come," I yelled at Harry.

"Shut up," he hissed back.

We waited tense fingers on the triggers, and when the horsemen reached the scrub cedar, Harry's bullet kicked up the dust in the trail before them. I looked over at the rock pile where Harry lay. A cloud of blue smoke was rising above him.

"Oh m'gosh!" I thought. "They'll see right where he is hid."

I looked back at the horsemen. They were arguing, and two of them seemed to be pulling their horses' heads, as if turning them back, but two others spurred their horses toward the gap. I sighted at a small bush and fired, the bullet kicked up the dust, and the horses halted. Now smoke was rising over my hiding place. I was in a panic. The six horsemen had all stopped. After a long pause, they turned and went down the trail single file. After they went around the point out of sight, we left our hiding places. Harry took Tuffy and fed and watered him. Then he took the saddle off. He said, "Tom wouldn't want the saddle left on all night."

Later Dad rode into camp and asked,

"See anything of Tom Dilly?"

Harry said, "Yes, he borrowed old Dunk."

"I see," Dad replied.

The next day, a rider came into camp. He and Dad discussed the fact that Steve Chipman (a sheepman) and Tom Dilley had had words in a saloon in Sunnyside. During the quarrel, Tom Dilley had shot Chipman, killing him. Dad had been in the saloon when the shooting occurred. When the sheriff called for a posse, he did not ask Dad to ride as he was aware that Tom and Dad were friends. When the posse was stopped at our Circle Dot camp, the sheriff assumed that Tom and his confederates had taken over while the camp owner was away, and no blame was ever attached to Dad. It was when Dad returned to camp that he learned his kids had supplied Tom with a fresh horse, but it was many years before he learned they had also supplied the delaying tactics that provided Tom with the needed start.[9]

Tom Dilley went to Vernal, Utah, then over Diamond Mountain to Brown's Park. From there he went to Rock Springs, Wyoming. Fresh horses

"The Chew Boys Road." A switch-back trail originally built with horses and fresno scrapers so cows could be driven into Pat's Hole. *Courtesy of Rene Chew Steele.*

were obtained at ranches as needed. They were returned to the owners by others traveling the return route.

That was how the Outlaw Trail worked for the criminal element.

In the spring and summer of 1910, Jack Chew and his son Harry, along with Clark Elmer, used both black powder and dynamite to widen and flatten a trail down into Pat's Hole. They spent many hours with a pick and crowbar smoothing out the trail so they could drift the cattle down to Pat's Hole and across the Yampa River.[10]

Doug Chew, a younger brother of Leath (Avvon), was born in Brown's Park in 1902. After he was grown, he homesteaded and ranched on Blue Mountain. His cattle range included parts of the Outlaw Trail. In 1971, he took several of his children and grandchildren through the Western Colorado portion of the Outlaw Trail. Rene Chew Steele shared the following account:

> *Grandpa* [Douglas] *Chew said that everyone had to be a good rider and eleven years old or older. Everyone met at Doug Chew's homestead cabin on Blue Mountain. On the first day, we saddled up and rode down the "Chew Boys Road" of switchbacks going down into Iron Springs….We rode past one of Pat Lynch's caves, and there were interesting remains, an old wood bed frame, some clothing and leather things….We meandered down to Ralph Chew's sod roofed cabin, past fields and irrigation ditches to the "Whispering Caves" and petroglyphs along the canyon walls. We ended up riding past Steamboat Rock to Echo Park. We spent the night there.* [The younger children and

the women took sleeping bags, groceries and trucks around to each camping spot.]

On the second day, Grandpa [Doug] Chew demonstrated how to swim his horse....He jumped his horse off the bank into the river, and both went out of sight. They came to the surface; Grandpa had slid off his horse along the side of him. Splashing water in his horse's face to make him swim the direction he wanted him to go. Eventually, Grandpa was holding onto the horse's tail. They came out of the river on the other side. Soon Grandpa jumped his horse into the river to swim back to us. He told us to "never get in front of the horse or he'll try to walk on you to get out of the water."

Grandpa took us to a shallow, safer place to ford the river. Water was past the horse's bellies. One horse was drifting downstream and Grandpa said to splash water in his face to get him to fight the current....

As we started up the Outlaw Trail, we had to traverse layers of slick rock; at one point, Uncle Harry's horse ended up on his back between two big rocks. It took a while to get his horse on his feet again....

Along the trail there were axe blazes to mark the way, other places that had been fixed to allow horses and pack horses to pass. There were holes bored into the rock and metal rods to hold poles, rocks and dirt to allow animals to walk around some steep edges of rock.

There were places in the steep slick rock that had been chipped out for horses to walk in for safer footing. (Scott told me that they built fires on the rocks where they wanted to chip; the heat helped to fracture the rocks easier.)

The Outlaw Trail crossed the river and traveled on a switch-back trail up the slick rock side of the canyon at the center of the photo. *Courtesy of Rene Steele.*

Aunt Enola, Grandpa's sister, told me that they would tie a pack horse's lead rope to the horse's tail in front of them. One time, one of her brother's pack horses hugged the ledge too close and lost his balance and fell to his death below, pulling the lead horse's tail off.... [It pulled the hair out of the tail.]

We looked off at Ladore Canyon then went on to Zenobia Basin across Douglas Mountain to Current Springs in Brown's Park, where Grandpa was born in a dugout. It took eight hours to make the ride from Steamboat Rock to Current Springs.[11]

Rene also believed that her family was possibly the last to travel along the Outlaw Trail, as portions of it caved off and slid into the Green River a year or so after they had ridden through.

ANOTHER STORY ABOUT THE getaway route was reported in 1905:

J.A. Wright, a prominent rancher of Axial, Routt County, Colorado was killed by an unknown person, on Monday. It is said that the unknown murderer walked up behind Wright and sent a bullet through his back, killing him instantly. Several persons witnessed the shooting, but none could identify the murderer, who made good his escape.[12]

Dave Gray told the next story about the early town of Egeria (now Yampa). The justice of the peace mentioned in this account was Dave Gray's father.

In 1883, Joe Ward came to settle what is now known as the VanCamp Cabins. He was a notorious character and his was the toughest outfit that ever came to Egeria Park....In the fall of 1884, Joe Ward killed Charles Fox. On the same day that the killing took place, Tom Gibbs was hunting horses on Watson Creek when he ran into two men butchering fat calves. Excitement in the community was high. It was discovered that these men were making a business of butchering and that Joe Ward was hauling the meat to Leadville to market. Mark Choate and L.L. Wilson arrested Ward. Because there was no jail, he was held under guard. Alex Gray, justice of the peace, acted as coroner. There was no question of Ward's guilt. Fox and Ward were of the same ilk, being equally undesirable. No tears were shed because of the loss of Fox, but there was some head-scratching among the citizens as to what to do with Ward. Courts, officers and jail were

Alex Grey's homestead. Charles Fox was buried about where the photographer was standing, circa 1910. *Yampa-Egeria Museum, Fogg Collection.*

so far away that prosecuting him was practically impossible. After some discussion it was decided to turn Ward loose on condition that he leave the country and never return. This he agreed to do. Charles Fox was buried on the hillside just west of Phippsburg.

Wards moved to Government Bridge on the Yampa River. A short time later, when Ward was on his way to Rawlins, Wyoming [with rustled cattle] *he was followed by a posse and shot to death. Ward's wife and their two children remained on the ranch at Government Bridge for a number of years. Clover, the Ward boy, was drowned when he ran his bicycle off the bridge into the river.*

Mrs. Ward was burned to death when the ranch house burned, and the girl, it was reported, died a disgraceful death. So ended the Ward chapter in the history of Northwestern Colorado.[13]

The following two stories were included in the local papers in 1905:

Sheriff Jones passed through here Saturday, having in charge the Vincent brothers, who last week pleaded guilty to horse stealing before District Judge Shumate, and were sentenced by the court to one to ten years in the state reformatory at Buena Vista. These are the same boys who, a short time ago, gave Sheriff Jones a chase into Grand County before they were captured. The boys stole two horses and saddles from Hayden. At Steamboat, being headed off by the town marshal, they abandoned their mounts, circled the town and got as far as Granby before they were apprehended. They were incarcerated at Hahn's Peak, where they attempted to escape by overpowering Deputy Sheriff McCormick and throwing him into the cell they had occupied. They were recaptured, however, and special term of court was called to try their case. If their conduct is first-class at the reformatory, they will get their liberty in about eleven months. [14]

Edward Dunckley, a young man from William's Park and a black sheep in a respected family, was held to the District court yesterday, upon a charge of forgery. He passed a check bearing the name of his brother, G.W. Dunckley, at the Antlers hotel for $13.75. Cashier Dart of the Bank of Yampa spotted the forged signature and Dunckley was arrested, whereupon he claimed to have authority to sign his brother's name. At the hearing before Justice Bayles, this was proven false and he was taken to Hahn's Peak to await trial, being unable to furnish bonds. C.A. Morning appeared as special district attorney. Dunckley is said to have also passed bad paper on two other business houses in town. [15]

The next incident was told by Francis Moore when he was talking about his Aunt Maude and Uncle Billy Macfarlane:

In 1937 or 1938 Billy Macfarlane was undersheriff when a "bad guy" [he had evidently pulled a holdup] *was running from the authorities The sheriff's office had called the adjoining counties and had set up road blocks. Anyway, the man had left Steamboat and was heading toward the south end of Routt County. During the night, Maurice Pidcock had heard a car trying to go up and over Greenridge. So, he told Billy that he was sure the man was trying to get out of the county that way. Billy Macfarlane stopped in the lane (Francis and Gladys Moore lived in a small house on what is now county road 21 from 1934 until 1937) and asked Francis if there was any way the fellow could get to Kremmling by going over Greenridge.*

Francis told him that he couldn't get through that way in a vehicle. The law enforcement officers caught the guy not long after near Toponas. He evidently had tried to escape by going over Greenridge. What Maurice

Pidcock had heard was the noise the man made when he couldn't make it through those trails and wagon tracks, turned around, and went back down the hill.[16]

This certainly does not include all the notorious stories or characters of the period. Though, it does give one the essence of the times. Many of the stories that might have been told were kept quiet. After all, the families in the area did not really want to admit that there might be a "black sheep" among them.

How They Arrived

The following stories tell how a few families arrived in the Yampa Valley in the thirty years between 1882 and 1912. The way those families survived is the origin of heroes. However, their stories seem to be representative of the many who came during that time.

The Bartz Family

In 1865, John Bartz emigrated from Germany to the United States through Ellis Island, when he was sixteen years old. He married Alice MaGinnis while he was still in New York. John developed miner's consumption (tuberculosis), so the doctors recommended the dry climate of Colorado.[17] The family moved to Georgetown. John worked as a bookkeeper for a large mining company and also learned some gold assaying skills. While they were in Georgetown, six of their seven children were born.

In 1889, John came to Routt County and took up a 160-acre homestead, 3.5 miles south of Sydney, Colorado, on Antelope Creek. Before he moved his family from Georgetown, John built a four-room house made of sawn lumber.

John and Alice were both "city people" and not familiar with driving a heavy team and wagon. When John bought a team in Georgetown, he got a team that was spoiled and balky. John had great difficulty getting the team

Mrs. Alice Bartz, circa 1900. *Herold family collection.*

started again when they balked going up a hill. Alice would not stay in the wagon when they came to a steep hill. She would get out and walk, leaving the oldest girl, Bess, in the wagon to hold the Baby, Orpha. They traveled through Dillon, down the Blue River to Kremmling, then over Gore Pass. After they reached Egeria Park, they had no more steep hills to go over, but the Morrison Creek area and Yellow Jacket Pass could get so muddy it "could mire a saddle blanket." On the journey from Georgetown to Sidney, they were only able to travel about ten to twelve miles a day. Which meant they spent twelve to fifteen days on the trail. Truly primitive conditions for a couple that had never camped in tents, cooked over an open fire, taken care of a team, or even managed five young children in the open country.

Proving up on their homestead was not any easier. Grubbing out sagebrush or driving an unwilling team to plow the ground took the labor of both adults. Alice drove the team as best as she could, while John handled the walking plow. The range cattle from the large cattle companies gathered around their house on Antelope Creek; their two-wire fence did nothing to stop the cows from entering their garden or oats patch. In spite of their problems, they were able to meet the requirements to obtain the deed for their land.[18]

28

When he first arrived in 1889, John and his partner, William Leninger, built a two-story building in Steamboat Springs on Lincoln and Eighth Streets.

It had a big oven built of stone and the inside was lined with metal. Leninger was a baker, his pies and cookies were great. The building in Steamboat had two large rooms on the lower floor, one for the bakery and the front room was for the store to sell the bakery goods. The upper rooms, which were five, were fixed for the family to live in.[19]

John Bartz still had investments in Georgetown; in 1895, he went to get some return on his money. While there, he had a flare-up of his tuberculosis. He tried to return to Steamboat Springs but died on the way home. He was buried in Salida, Colorado.

Alice sold the homestead and started the Bartz Hotel in their Steamboat bakery and house. That rooming house served three meals a day to both boarders and drop-in customers. All the daughters were expected to help clean, cook and serve the food at the family-style meals. Josephine, the third girl, said she had to leave school to serve the noon meal and was often late returning to her classes. Alice ran both the Bartz Hotel and her family with an iron fist. She wanted her children to be "true ladies and a gentleman." The five girls took piano lessons and learned to paint with watercolors. At the time his father died, the only boy, twelve-year-old Ralph, was not allowed to do any arduous activities. Alice would not even let Ralph milk the cow as she was afraid that he might get hurt or that the cow "would not let her milk down."[20]

When John and Alice's children were of school age, some of them attended grade school in Sydney before moving into Steamboat Springs. Most of their children at least finished high school. Some of them went on to higher education.

THE ALBERT BIRD FAMILY

James Albert Bird was the eldest child of William and Mary Bird. The Bird family hauled freight between the mines in Breckenridge, Colorado, and the mines in Cripple Creek. Albert came into Egeria Park with his father looking for a horse thief, and he recognized the opportunity to obtain homesteads. Albert and his brothers, Tom and Lewis, returned to the South Routt area in 1881 to build cabins. In 1883, Albert traveled to

Missouri to marry Alice Browne. Together they returned to Routt County, so Albert could work both on his homestead and in the family sawmill before winter.

Around 1904, Albert built a slaughterhouse about one mile north of Yampa. At the time of this writing, the building is still standing. Albert had an agreement with George Canant to supply beef for Canant's stores.[21] Canant's first market was located on Moffat Avenue in Yampa. One store (currently called Crossan's M&A Market) was located in the large building just across Main Street from the present Yampa Museum; another, the Sanitary Market, was located on Sharp Street in Oak Creek.

Alice Brown Bird, wife of Albert Bird of Yampa, circa 1890. *Herold family collection.*

When Albert butchered the animals, he saved the feet, tossing them into a pile. When he had accumulated a large pile, he put them into a vat to boil them down. In this manner, he was able to make his own neatsfoot oil. This oil was very good for treating and preserving leather.

Albert butchered a large number of hogs. One of the steps in butchering hogs requires dipping the hogs into a large vat of scalding water. The scalding process releases the hair and bristles on a hog so the hide can be scraped clean. Albert was very good at finding that temperature without using a thermometer. Albert would draw his first finger slowly across the width of the tank. The water was the right temperature when it was so hot that he could not keep his finger in the water any longer than it took to move it from one side of the vat to the other. For scalding water to work correctly, it had to be just under the boiling point.[22]

When Albert got older, he became disabled and quite "stove up."[23] (He evidently had arthritis and grew more incapacitated each year.) George Canant hired Fred Orr to help Albert run the slaughterhouse.

Francis Moore recalled, "When I knew Albert, he was an 'old man.' I don't remember him riding a horse; he always walked. Because Albert was quite crippled, he would use two canes as he walked; he always walked from his house to the slaughterhouse each day to work [about a quarter of a mile]. For him to walk down the road he would 'sprawl' those canes out to the side."[24]

Albert Bird's slaughter house, northwest of Yampa, 1985. *Herold family collection.*

When Francis was seventeen or so, a cow got out of Albert's corral at the slaughterhouse. Carey Trantham (Albert's grandson) came to get Francis to help round up that cow. Francis was riding Tinker, a little mare that he had just gotten. Carey and Francis had quite a time getting that cow out of the meadow and back into Albert's corral; "she certainly did not want to go."

The newspaper had this to say about Albert Bird: "The Routt-Moffat Pioneer Picnic was held in VanCamp's Grove on July 1, 1933. Albert Bird of Yampa, one of the old timers, was too feeble to attend the entire meeting. He came to the Grove later in the afternoon and sat in a car while he talked to some of his friends."[25]

THE HEROLD FAMILY

Edward Herold and his family (wife Emma and the younger children, Edna, Irene, Clara and Carl) traveled by wagon from Denver, Colorado, to Pleasant Valley in the late fall of 1910.[26] The trip took them eight days, as they were traveling with an oversized freight wagon; the wheels were wider than the average wagon. It was much harder to hold in the tracks when traveling over the mountain passes. Their first two nights were spent along the road to get to the foot of Berthoud Pass. After getting to the west side of the pass, they expected to buy food at the next town, Fraser, but since it was Sunday, all the stores were closed. They went several more miles before they stopped to light a fire in the heavy rain. Emma was eventually able to get "sour" biscuits cooked so the family finally ate "beans and twenty-six biscuits."

The Herolds went over a "terrible steep mountain" before they got to Kremmling. They all got out of the wagon and walked up the hill for three hours before arriving at the summit. [The road skirted Byers Canyon.] *That night, they were able to stay with friends on the Troublesome River. Gore Pass was the next obstacle that came before them. Again, the family needed to walk behind the wagon, this time carrying rocks to place behind the wheels so the wagon would not roll backwards when the horses stopped to rest. It took a day and a half to get the wagon over that pass. Before that tired family arrived at Pleasant Valley, the last night was spent in their tent about a mile north of Yampa. In the night, a "mouse"* [probably a weasel] *got into the birdcage with Emma's canary and killed the "poor bird."*

The oldest boy, Julius, remained in Denver for several days. He and the family's household goods then traveled in an "immigrant car" over the Moffat Railroad to Sidney, Colorado. The furniture was taken to the train tracks by a "real good moving-van man" and loaded into one half of the car. Six cows and three lambs were loaded into the other half of the car. Three, two by six, boards were nailed into place to keep the animals in their half of the car. None of the family, or their friends, knew that they needed to place bedding (straw or gravel) on the floor of the railroad car for the animals.

When going over Corona Pass the train could not keep up enough pressure to keep the engines moving, so the train would stop to build up steam. Julius said that there were two engines in front, one in the middle and one at the end of the train. Each time when the engines started,

Julius Herold in 1918. *Herold family collection.*

they would "hit it" at different times to start the pull. Julius told a young brakeman that the engineers must be trying to kill him. "I was sitting on the wash machine and they hit it so hard that I went head first under the planks that held the cows in."[27]

When the train got to Hot Sulphur Springs, Julius was able to water the stock by placing a washtub in the car and carrying water from the river in a five-gallon bucket. By the time that immigrant car arrived in Sidney, Colorado, the floor of the car was "as slick as a ballroom floor." After thirty-three hours on the train, both Julius and the animals were definitely glad to reach their destination.

The family stayed at John Bonard's ranch for three months while they built their first cabin.[28] The women stayed in the house with the Bonards, while the men all slept in the hayloft over the barn. It was not unusual for the boys, Julius and Carl, to place their wet overalls beside the bed at night and then crawl into the solidly frozen pant legs the next morning.

In July 1916, Ed received the title to land in Pleasant Valley. Two or three years later, Ed sold the Pleasant Valley homestead and bought a tract of land farther south on the Yampa River, where he had more meadows for hay and grain. With the help of his children, he milked cows and made butter

Herold family. *Back row, left to right*: Julius, Carl; *front row*: Clara, Edna and Irene, circa 1955. *Herold family collection.*

and cheese to sell to the miners in Oak Creek. He carved a butter mold with his initials inscribed into it. That branded each pound of butter as his. The town residents soon found that he sold good, clean dairy products. His specialty was big rounds of longhorn cheese.

In 1921, Ed Herold and Bert Barrows co-owned a threshing machine.[29] This machine let the farmers living near the mouth of Sarvis Creek Canyon harvest their own grain. In December 1927, the snow caught the Barrowses' threshing machine at Julius Herold's ranch.[30] (That ranch was on the south shore of what is now Stagecoach reservoir.)

In 1924, after their children were all adults, Ed and Emma once more sold their Routt County land and moved back to Buffalo, New York, where Ed's brothers and sisters still resided. Three of Ed and Emma's five children remained in Colorado and raised families of their own.

THE LAUGHLIN FAMILY

Robert Laughlin moved his wife and two young sons from Missouri to a small divide just east of Colorado Springs, Colorado. Missouri was torn by the aftermath of the Civil War.

All this small family owned was a wagon, a handful of household items and a few head of horses. One of those horses was a stallion, Nick.[31] Nick and several other horses had been taken from Tennessee during the last few weeks of the Civil War.

In 1885, Robert decided to move again; by now, there were three more children added to his family. This time, they would take their wagons, horses and cows to Egeria Park in Routt County. His wife's cousins, the Birds, had settled there three years before.

The trip from Colorado Springs to Egeria Park took about three weeks. The way was rough and rocky. The roads were nothing but trails and more rocks. Frances (Robert's wife) later made the comment that one blessing from the rocky road was "the butter never had to be churned." They put the cream in a container on the back of one of the wagons, and it would be churned by the evening camp.

Another problem the family faced on the trip was the cattle got sore feet from the sharp rocks. The animals' hooves became worn down, and they did not want to travel. Robert had extra horseshoes along, so he decided to shoe the cattle. To do that, the shoes had to be cut in half to fit the cloven hoofs. The animals that were sore footed had to be roped and tied down

Mabel and Bertha
Laughlin, about 1885.
Herold family collection.

before the split shoes were nailed on each toe. That was a strenuous and time-consuming activity.[32]

Frances related another story about that trip from Colorado Springs to the Yampa Valley:

> *One of the hardest parts of any journey by wagon was the crossing of rivers. The Grand River (now the Colorado River) was considered one of the most dangerous rivers in the west. The fast, cold, deep water made extremely treacherous undertows. Robert and the two oldest boys, Walter and Ben, drove the horses and cows across. The hired man drove the front wagon and Frances drove the last wagon. Before they started, Robert told Frances to follow the first wagon across the river. The three smaller children rode behind the seat of Frances's wagon. The oldest girl, Bertha, held the baby, age two, on her lap.*

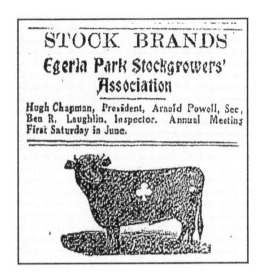

The Laughlin family was involved in the cattle industry for many years. Ben Laughlin served as the brand inspector. *From the* Yampa Leader, *September 15, 1913.*

When she was out in the middle of the river, Frances started watching that fast, muddy water roll around her. She started screaming, "We're floating down stream! We're floating down steam!"

Robert rode up alongside of the wagon and roared, "Old Woman, watch the wagon in front of you, not the water." That was enough to snap Frances's attention from the water. She wasn't really floating downstream— she started following the other wagon and made it across the river just fine. In later years, Frances would comment, "That was one time I was glad he [Robert] yelled at me."

After arriving in Egeria Park, they moved to a place originally built by Ed Watson. This was located just east of the present-day Yampa Cemetery. Five more children (Maude, Bob, Gordon, Ruth and Theresa) were born there. The family was active in the community, and the children grew up and had homes of their own. Walter, Ben, Bertha and Tom all applied for homesteads as soon as they were old enough and proved up on them. The men raised both cattle and horses for a living.

THE MARGERUM FAMILY

Charles Elmer Margerum brought his wife, Shirley, and their three-year-old daughter, Gladys, to Routt County in 1913.[33] Elmer moved from Oklahoma because his in-laws, the Hunicks, had described a place west of the Hunick homestead that Elmer could "prove up on." Elmer homesteaded that place, eight miles west of Yampa, Colorado near the Little Flattops.

He soon had twenty-two milk cows. He would milk before daylight, place the cans of milk in a wagon and take it to Oak Creek to sell to the company stores at the mines. He would then fill the wagon with a load of coal to haul back to whoever might need it in the Yampa area. He also shipped milk and cream on the train to Steamboat Springs or Denver.

In those first years, if he was not hauling milk toward Oak Creek during the winter, he would milk the cows then go and work in the Bird sawmill that was west of his homestead. Of course, after his daytime work, no matter where it was, the cows always needed to be milked when he got home.

In 1921, Elmer moved his family (they had added another daughter, Thelma) into the town of Yampa. He started hauling oil and gasoline for the Continental Oil Company; he did this for the next forty-two years. When he first started hauling gasoline and oil, he used a tank on a wagon and pulled it with a team of horses. This team and wagon might be seen in the McCoy area one day or in the Dunkley Pass area the next. As the demand for oil and gasoline increased, Elmer updated his transportation to trucks.

In back: Shirley and Elmer Margerum; *in front*: daughters Thelma and Gladys at their homestead house, about 1916. *Herold family collection.*

Even while he was working for the Conoco Oil Company, Elmer did many other jobs on the side. He co-owned and helped run the M&M Garage; this was located east of the Antler's Café on Moffat Avenue. Elmer acquired the contract for the mail route that went from Yampa to the many families who lived west of Yampa; that route extended to the Pinnacle Post Office. When they were in high school, his daughters, Gladys and Thelma, often ran this route for him.

Until 1960, the school bus was privately owned. In 1928, Elmer bought the first bus to carry the children from Hunt Creek to the

Elmer (C.E.) Margerum drove the school bus from Yampa to Trout Creek, then to Phippsburg, letting off the elementary students. He loaded any high school kids on the bus and returned to Yampa each morning. After school, the route was reversed. Viola Iacovetto standing in front, 1942. *Historical Society of Oak Creek and Phippsburg.*

Phippsburg School. He then carried the high school students to the Union High School in Yampa. He drove that route for nearly thirty years.

In 1928, Elmer became the first 4-H leader in South Routt County; it was the Yampa Dairy Calf Club. Those first 4-H members included Walter Bennett, Eileen Elgin, Fred Elgin, Leo Hawley, Buford Huffstetler, Dan Knott, Thelma Margerum and Walter Peters.

About the same time, he helped with the Camp Fire Girls by taking them on camping trips. Once, they spent nearly a week going over the Flattops to Trappers Lake and back. They camped and fished both directions.

Elmer and his family remained in Yampa for many years.

THE MONTGOMERY FAMILY

Ilda Montgomery was the granddaughter of William and Louisa Montgomery. When Ilda was in high school during the early 1920s, she won second prize in a writing contest for the following article:

If at any time you have read a story of a pioneer and thought that the hardships and deprivations were greatly exaggerated, I ask you to listen to the stories of some of our pioneers of the Yampa Valley, who endangered their lives and property to advance the frontier of civilization. Among the few remaining pioneers of the vicinity of Yampa is Mrs. [Louisa] Montgomery who located on what is now the Dr. Cole ranch about one-half mile southeast of Yampa, November 3, 1882. She tells the following story.

My husband and I with our four children came from Kokoma, Colorado, over what is now the Gore road. From Kokoma we came to Dillon on the stage. At Dillon we hired two men and teams to bring us on over. The trail, which had not been traveled for some time, had to be recut and progress was slow. There was a heavy snow, and as we were loaded too heavy, we left part of our provisions on top of the range.

Mr. Montgomery on a previous trip to this country had built a small one room cabin, but as lumber was not obtainable, it did not have a floor.

When we arrived the night of November 3, there was no snow, but the next morning everything was white and remained so until late in the spring.

Our only worry that winter was to get settled and to keep the wolf from our door. Because contrary to nearly every one's ideas of pioneer life there were no Indians here, as we came the year after the Indian Massacre of Meeker and all the Indians had been driven out of the county. There was an abundance of wild game, and we had plenty of bread, but vegetables were very scarce, we only brought six hundred pounds of potatoes, most of which we had to keep to plant, and a small amount of canned goods.

For some time after we came a wash tub and boiler was our table. We bought some lumber at Elk River for sixty dollars a thousand and paid a man five dollars a day to get it out, we then floored the cabin.

The next spring, we cleared twenty-five acres of land by hand, because we did not get a team until late in the year 1883, and people who had teams asked such high prices for their labor that we could not afford to hire help. In the latter part of June 1883, we had cleared enough ground for a garden. A short time later there was a great freeze which froze all the gardens but ours. That left a scarcity of feed, because it was impossible to get to Denver until late in July for supplies.

But in early days what belonged to one was shared by everyone. And let me also add she has not forgotten the spirit of fellowship.[34]

William Montgomery homesteaded on what was then the main road south of Yampa (now County Road 6D). He and his wife, Louisa, had three daughters and one son, Merrill. Their eldest child, Charlotte, was eight years old when they came to Routt County. The youngest, Merrill, was two. The

Mervin, Ilda, Bertha, Bernice and Joe, Lulu and Merrill Montgomery's children, about 1915. *Herold family collection.*

girls (Charlotte, Catherine and Eva) cleared the rocks from the meadow near their house.[35] That rock pile made a formidable heap at the edge of the meadow. Two of the Montgomery girls, Catherine and Eva, married the two Arnold boys, Harry and Charley.

Merrill married Lulu Orr. They had a small ranch just east of Yampa, then moved into Yampa, where Lulu raised their five children (Joe, Ilda, Mervin, Bertha and Bernice) after Merrill died.

Some of the Montgomery family still reside in Yampa; as of this writing, they own and operate the Montgomery's General Merchandise.

THE NAY FAMILY

In 1880, Marshall Nay traveled from Kansas in a covered wagon to Denver with his family, wife Emma, Ida (seven), William (five) and Samuel (three).[36] The trip took about one month. Emma worried about the children being bitten by a rattlesnake or getting lost. Marshall worried about the wagon breaking down or the team straying and the crossing of rivers and gullies.

There were no bridges, so Marshall would drive carefully crossing the gullies. Sometimes the wagon ruts were unevenly tilted on the side of a bank and it would be difficult to stay on the wagon seat or even keep the seat on the wagon box. It was always a worry that the water barrel would tip or break loose from the wagon bed. Once the slope was greater than Marshall thought and the water barrel almost broke loose, so Marshall stopped the team and got back to the barrel and held onto it until Emma drove to a level place. Emma did not like it, but she was certainly able to drive the team.

The Nay family did not stay in Denver very long. Marshall went to Morrison, Colorado, and bought a small grocery and meat market. This business kept Marshall very busy, as he ran the store by himself and did the butchering of the meat in the evenings. The boys were expected to help from a very young age. Not only were they to work in the shop, cleaning and helping to butcher the animals, but they also helped herd the small flock of sheep that Marshall kept. The sheep supplied mutton for the Nays' own table and for sale in the market. To break the tedium of work, the boys grew up playing baseball. Will was the catcher for the Morrison town team, and Sam was the pitcher; games were played on Sunday afternoons.

In 1891, Marshall moved to Altman, a mining camp just outside Cripple Creek, Colorado. Will and Sam were still in their teens, but Ida was married there. Again, Marshall opened a meat market and grocery store, M.M. Nay and Sons. In the 1890s, Will married and had two children, Marshall W. and Clara. Both Will and Sam worked full time in the meat market.

Because of the extreme trouble between the mine owners and the miners' union during the late 1890s, Marshall once more moved—this time to the Yampa Valley. In his later years, Sam told about his horseback ride into Steamboat Springs. It was in the spring of 1903; he rode over the passes that still had snow drifts two and three feet high. But the mud was the biggest problem. Sam was twenty-four years old; his only possessions were a horse, a saddle, forty dollars and one change of clothing.

Sam bought the Altmon Grocery Store and Meat Market in Steamboat Springs with a handshake and a promise to pay the former owner. Sam then hired Clem (C.N.) Smith to run the store, while he bought and sold cattle. At about the same time, both Sam and Will Nay filed on homesteads in the Sidney area. Will filed west of Sidney and Sam south of Sidney. In 1905, the Nays bought a "house on Crawford hill" in Steamboat Springs. Marshall M. Nay lived there for a time.

Verna Bartz, Sam Nay and Josephine Bartz, about 1907. *Herold family collection.*

In 1905, Sam Nay, Charles Temple, J.L. Norvell and J.N. McWilliams took 240 head of cattle to the train at Wolcott for shipment to Denver. As was customary at the time, the cattlemen rode in the caboose on the cattle train to the market.

> *While in Denver, Sam Nay was awarded the contract for providing the meat to the laborers of the Moffat Railroad while the tracks were laid from Kremming to Steamboat Springs, Colorado. Both Sam and Will Nay butchered cattle and delivered the meat to the railroad construction crews. This meant that they were in Yampa as often as they were in Steamboat Springs. Sam especially kept the road warm as he rode back and forth while he courted Josephine Bartz. He and Josephine got married in 1907. They spent the next year at the Gibbs ranch just south of Finger Rock near Yampa.*
>
> *Sam and Will Nay both remained in Routt County with their families for many years after they became established.*[37]

The right to homestead land seems to be the common element that brought these families to Routt County. Some sold their homesteads as soon as they obtained the deed to the ground and used the profit to start other enterprises. Others, like the Will Nay family and the Laughlin family, were able to cut hay and raise enough livestock to pass the land down to future generations. The early pioneers came over trails and rudely formed roads. Several of the later settlers came by train, but their goals were the same. Some of those early settlers were dreamers; some were just strongminded businessmen and women, but all of them were seeking a future for their families.

3

PEOPLE

T he following short sketches do not include all of the early pioneers of the area. The information and stories were obtained from multiple sources. These are not biographies; most are accounts that I have not seen in other books or manuscripts. These vignettes are intended to add insight and information about the people who lived here and add to the existing knowledge of the valley.

ELI AREOLA

Eli Areola lived on the "River Road" (Routt County Road No. 7) about a half mile southeast of Yampa.[38] He put up the fence and did chores for his neighbor, "the widow woman" Brownie Murry. She always referred to him as "Mistah" Areola. Later, he moved about a mile northwest of Yampa. After the two-story brick school was built in 1924, Areola moved the small one-story school to County Road 17. It is still in use as a private residence. Mr. Areola's son, Clyde, married Bob Laughlin's daughter, Dorphine.

ALFRED FAMILY: JIM ALFRED

Jim Alfred settled on a place up the Bear River Road. "It was the house that sat just to the side as you cross the river the second time."[39] Jim Alfred died just about the time that his eldest son, Lawrence "Lee," was a senior in high

Above: Skiing was not only fun but also transportation to the schoolhouse. The Alfred children circa 1915. *Yampa-Egeria Museum.*

Left: Howard, Florence and Lila Allen at their homestead, about 1926, *Herold family collection.*

school. The other sons were Bruce, a junior that year (around 1923) and Elmer, who was a couple years younger. Their daughter, Betty, was about the same age as Lee. About the time Elmer finished school, Lillian E. Alfred sold the place up the river road and moved the boys to the Joe Johnson place, on Greenridge about two miles north of Yampa.

LILA ALLEN

Lila Egeria Crossan was the first white child to be born in Upper Egeria Park, on May 25, 1885. When she was grown, she married Howard Allen. When they first married, they lived on a homestead about seven miles west of Yampa. Later, Lila helped Howard run a general mercantile store in Yampa (The M&A Market). Lila was an active member of the Yampa Women's Club and a popular member of the Yampa community.

MIKE BENEDICT

Mike and his wife, Emily, owned the Antler's Café and Bar for many years after World War II. During the 1950s and 1960s, this became the gathering place for locals, both the outlying ranchers and the town residents. Mike would not tolerate any fighting in his establishment. If people got unruly, he would kick them out, as he was his own bouncer. In his later years, Mike and his dog could be seen each morning as they crossed Moffat Avenue to the post office to get the mail.

FRANK BIRD

Frank Bird was one of William and Mary Ellen's children. Frank Bird's house and barns were where Yampa is located; this land was sold or donated to the Yampa School District.[40] The house and barns were built on the block that now contains the school. The house stood where the bus barn is now located. By the time, Francis Moore was in the third grade (about 1918); the house was moved south to a location about one mile west of Finger Rock. When Francis was in the lower elementary grades, the boys would take their lunches outside to eat; they would often stand near the old Bird barn, which had not yet been moved. Francis said that the barn had been chinked with manure to fill in the spaces between the logs. Anna Bird's handprints could still be seen in the cow manure chinking. By the time Francis was in the fourth grade, the barn had been moved from the school grounds.

GEORGE RILEY BIRD

Riley Bird was a son of Robert Bird and Jane Wilson Bird. He was a first cousin to the William Bird family.

According to the stories told about "Uncle Riley," he did not like to hurry but made every move count. The work he performed was of excellent quality, but to an onlooker, he sometimes appeared to be lazy because he seemed to move so slowly.

One year, Uncle Riley was helping Robert Laughlin, Riley's brother-in-law, dig his potatoes. They had worked for three or four days, and there were still many potatoes to be dug. Uncle Riley asked if Robert had enough potatoes dug to feed his family for the winter.

"Well, yes, but we can't leave the rest in the ground," Robert answered.

"I'll help any man dig potatoes to feed their family, but I won't dig potatoes for selling," stated Riley. Riley then went home without digging any more.

Another story told about Uncle Riley, was regarding the work for Bruce Roupe. Riley was mowing hay for $ 2.00 a day. Each day he would get to Bruce Roupe's place and pick up a sickle that someone else had sharpened, get the horses and go out to mow. At that time, most men sharpened their own sickles in the evening when they came in from the fields. Therefore, Bruce thought it was a little unfair that Riley didn't grind his own sickles. The next year, Riley wanted to mow for Bruce Roupe; he then asked what the going wages were for a mower.

"Well—" drawled Mr. Roupe, "It's $2.00 for a man who just mows, and $2.50 for a man who also sharpens his own sickles."

That year, Uncle Riley sharpened his own sickles.

Riley had lots of patience and was quite good at irrigating hay; his hay fields always produced a high yield. When he was asked what his secret was, he replied, "Anybody can irrigate if they don't try to make water run uphill." Some of his success was because he had the patience to lean on his shovel and wait for the water to cover the ground where it was needed before moving to a new location.

MABEL LINDSEY BIRD

Mabel Lindsey married Loren Bird, youngest son of William and Mary, and became known to all the children of the area as "Aunt Mabel." If the weather was bad, she would always let the kids come into her house and "cut and paste" or make newspaper puppets on her kitchen floor. The paste was a mixture of flour and water. The children usually managed to get a soft homemade cookie before they went home.

Mabel (Lindsey) Bird, circa 1950. *Herold family collection.*

WILLIAM BIRD

William and his wife, Mary (Wilson), came to the Yampa area in 1882. They built their homestead cabin just south of their son Albert's cabin. They raised a large family at this location. The people of the entire area called William Bird either "Bill" or else "Grandpa" Bird.[41]

When Grandpa Bird decided to retire and move to town, the local newspaper had this to say: "Grandpa Bird has shaken the ranch where he has been a resident for 23 years, placing the management thereof in the hands of his son, General Ulysses S. Grant Bird, and has moved into his new residence at the corner of Main Street and Roosevelt Avenue."[42]

A few days later this article appeared: "Grandpa Bird is working away at his house on North Main Street and when he gets it finished, it will be one of the best in the country."[43]

> *William Bird…first established a residence in Colorado in 1875, and at what is now the town of Yampa in 1880.*
>
> *Grandpa and Grandma Bird as they are most affectionately called by their many friends and neighbors now live in a cozy little home in Yampa where they extend the same hospitable welcome to all comers that in an early day made the Bird ranch a popular place in the days when the freight teams, the snow shoe and the saddle horse were the only means of transportation. Grandpa Bird is now in his 78th year and Grandma is a few years younger.*
>
> *The boys of the family…are James, known as Albert, Louis, John Frank, Ulysses, Robert and Earnest Loren.…Of the girls Mrs. Samantha Laramore lives near Sidney and Mrs. Della McCoy lives near Yampa.*[44]

GEORGE CANANT

George Canant had an interest in two or three meat markets and grocery stores in Yampa. His last location was in the building now known as the Crossan's M&A Market. That store sat directly across Main Street from the Bank of Yampa (now the Yampa-Egeria Museum). Canant also owned a store in Oak Creek, the Sanitary Grocery.[45]

George Canant hired Albert Bird to furnish the meat that was sold in his various mercantile stores. George Canant would buy live animals, and Albert would slaughter and process them. Canant would sometimes buy several animals at a time. They would stay in a pasture near the slaughterhouse until they were needed. Occasionally, the pigs would get out and start rooting and digging up the meadow. Canant would say, "That's okay, the meadow was getting sod bound."

Albert Bird made this comment, "Some people have got it in for George, but he has been all right with me." Francis Moore also remarked that Canant seemed to be fair with people.

George Canant is wearing a white apron; this store was in the west wing of the Royal Hotel before the hotel's addition, circa 1905. *Yampa-Egeria Museum.*

W.W. CARLE

In the *Steamboat Pilot*'s anniversary edition, Judge Morning had this to say about W.W. Carle: "Judge W.W. Carle was the postmaster when I first located at Yampa. He was for many years justice of the peace and also did much of the law business there during early days."[46]

Herb Moore always chuckled when he told the following story:

> *The elk moved out of the upper valley in the fall; they went down toward the Craig and Maybell area to winter where there wasn't as much snow. This annual migration took place before the weather got cold enough for the early settlers to get their winter's meat and keep it frozen so it would not spoil. After it got cold each year the men would take several wagons and go to an area west of Craig to shoot enough meat to supply their families until spring. The last year they went down to get their elk; the State had passed a law that there was to be hunting by license only and each person could only harvest one animal. This was not enough to get the early settlers by for the winter, as most of them had large families, so they ignored the new law and went anyway.*

Judge and Mrs. Carle, circa 1905. *Yampa-Egeria Museum.*

The large group of settlers from Yampa included Herb Moore, Walter Laughlin, and Judge Carle. All the fellows were a bit unhappy about Judge Carle going along because someone else had to shoot his animals for him, as Judge Carle was a terrible shot. After they shot enough animals to last the winter, they loaded the wagons and started home. One of the fellows that had been riding his horse ahead of the wagons, rode back in a big hurry. The game wardens had set up a roadblock in a narrow canyon to catch and stop the hunters.

Judge Carle said, "Don't worry boys; I'll take care of this." He rode up to the game wardens and told them, "It's all right fellows, I've already got them under arrest. I'm just taking them back home to try them. We have to take the meat as evidence."

With that, they traveled back to Yampa. When they got to Yampa, Judge Carle held court and fined them all a dollar, then sent them on their way. Needless to say, they were all happy that they had taken Judge Carle along, even if they did have to shoot his animals for him.[47]

That was the last year that the people from the Yampa area took their wagons "to the lower country" to get their winter's meat. After that, most of the residents shot the one or two animals that the law allowed and started eating more beef.

HENRY CRAWFORD

Henry Crawford built a homestead cabin on the hill just south of where the Yampa Cemetery is now located. It is possible that the cabin was actually located in the corner of the present-day cemetery.

The first school board meeting for Egeria School District No. 6 was held in Crawford's cabin on May 1, 1883.[48] The first school directors were Alex Gray, Mark Choate and William Bird.

Dave Gray said that Henry Crawford was killed in 1882.[49] Gray was not sure whether Mrs. Crawford was a resident of the cabin at the time the school board convened or not, but she was evidently elsewhere during the summer, as the cabin was used for the first school in Egeria Park. Another building was constructed before the next school term. Lulita Pritchett also mentioned that Henry Crawford was an early resident in the Egeria Park area.[50]

GEORGE CROSSAN, ROBERT CROSSAN

George Cooke Crossan came to Upper Egeria and built his first cabin in 1882.[51] The next spring, George brought his wife, Rachel, and their three children, Clyde, Charles and Myrtie (Macfarlane), to Upper Egeria Park. Cattle and hay seemed to be the major business of this family. George and Rachel had two more children born in Routt County.

Robert "Bob" Crossan was born on December 12, 1893. Bob was in the first class of students to graduate from the Yampa High School. For several years, Bob was a partner with his brother-in-law, Howard Allen, in the M&A Market in Yampa. Bob and his son George ran the store for a number of years after Howard Allen retired, until they decided it was time to retire in 1964.

LAWRENCE DAVIS

During the 1920s and 1930s, Lawrence Davis came to Yampa to visit his uncle Herb Moore. He stayed and worked in the hayfields and worked in the sawmills. He and his many cousins, including Earle Moore, Gordon Laughlin and Cecil Long, were all young men, and many jokes and tricks were played on one another. Lawrence left the area and joined the U.S. Navy.

CLYDE ELGIN

Clyde Elgin was raised by the Lindseys; his ride to school each day was at least ten miles. He started his ride each day "up the Bear River" about eight miles southwest of Yampa on what is now Routt County Road No. 7. He was one of the students that attended school where the present-day Yampa Cemetery is located.

TOM GIBBS, MARGARET GIBBS

Tom and Margaret Gibbs came into Egeria Park between 1882 and 1885. They settled just south of Finger Rock on what was later known as the Doc Marshal place. Margaret was the daughter of Arch Bird. Like many of the other early settlers, they lived in a log house for the first several years. After he became established, Tom built a large two-story house.

Above: Robert "Bob" Crossan, Howard Allen and Lila Allen inside the M&A Market, circa 1945. *Yampa-Egeria Museum.*

Left: Margaret & Tom Gibbs, circa 1900. *Yampa-Egeria Museum.*

E.H. GODFREY, LETTIE GODFREY

A resident of Yampa for several years, E.H. (Eugene or Gene) Godfrey was well known throughout the county for being the editor for the *Yampa Leader*. Not long after the newspaper building on Main Street in Yampa burned, Godfrey moved his newspaper to Oak Creek.

When they lived in Yampa, the E.H. Godfrey family lived in a house in the area that was called VanCamp Grove.[52] Both E.H. and Lettie Godfrey had strong personalities and believed in saying what they thought. One time the Moore family was eating supper with the Godfreys; Mrs. Godfrey decided she wanted more cupboards in her kitchen area. She once again started mentioning the need for cupboards, when Mr. Godfrey interrupted in an exasperated tone of voice, "Mother! We've added on to the house on every side except the side toward the barn, I guess we could probably add on there."

E.H. (Eugene) Godfrey and his printing press, located on Moffat Avenue in Yampa, circa 1910. *Historical Society of Oak Creek and Phippsburg.*

GRAY FAMILY: ALEX GRAY, DAVE GRAY, JACK GRAY, CECIL GRAY

Alex Gray came into Egeria Park in 1883. He was a cousin to William Bird. Alex Gray's homestead was located where the town of Phippsburg is now. Dave Gray was a son of that first settler and moved to Egeria Park as a child. Later, Dave Gray lived on a ranch about four miles southwest of Phippsburg.

Jack Gray lived on the river road southeast of Yampa (now County Road No. 7). He had two children, Cecil and Effie.

Cecil Gray worked for H.E. "Herb" Moore in the timber and on the ranch. Cecil and Francis Moore were good friends. Cecil was quite good at playing the harmonica; he "played by ear" and could play anything he had ever heard. When Francis asked him how he had learned to play so well, Cecil told him that they had had a hired hand that camped in a tent during haying time. (Evidently, that was a common practice during haying. Those working in the hay field could stay in the tents during the warm season and not crowd the family in the cabins.) He had an old "mouth harp," and Cecil's younger sister picked it up and played a tune that could be recognized. Cecil told Francis that he decided that if Effie could, so could he. He then started to practice and play.

A few years later after working in the timber, Cecil Gray was the overseer for the county road crew. Cal Thomas was the regular maintainer (road grader) operator.[53] There was too much snow one year for Cal to plow it out of the road. He had piled it so high that he couldn't push it any farther. Cecil knew that Francis Moore had run a cat with a front blade, so Cecil asked Francis to push the snow wider away from the roads. Francis did that for about three months. At that time, the county crew covered the entire south end of the county from Phippsburg to McCoy and even to the top of Gore Pass. Francis plowed each day from before daylight until dark. He covered the county roads from Toponas to Phippsburg; this included what the state highway department now plows. Of course, Cal was still using the maintainer and pushed the snow out of the middle of the roads.

One of the places that Francis plowed was the road into Dave Gray's place. Suzy Moore (no relation to any of the other Moores in the Yampa area) caught Francis and asked him why he had not plowed her road. She was quite indignant that her place was still snowed in. She lived above Dave

Gray's place, in the "saddle" over the hill on the way to Oak Creek. Francis told her that he just plowed the roads that Cecil told him to plow. Since she was the only one on that road, she was one of the last people to get her road plowed each time it snowed.

DICK GREENWOOD, MARY GREENWOOD

When Dick and Mary Greenwood were living at their place on Greenridge, H.E. Moore boarded with them occasionally during the winter. This would have been when H.E. was working in the timber on Greenridge.[54]

H.E. told about eating breakfast with them when Barry, their son, was just crawling. Barry would be in the kitchen while Mary was cooking breakfast. Mary would leave the door to the kitchen open and didn't worry about Barry crawling outside onto the porch. H.E. said that Barry would go outside, sit on the porch and look around. When he got "blue with the cold," he would crawl back into the kitchen.

After the Greenwoods moved into Yampa, Dick Greenwood coached the first basketball team for the school kids. One evening, both Dick and Mary were at the school, and he needed something from his house. He sent Francis Moore and Melvin Burris up to his house on Moffat Avenue (just east of the Hernage Store). Dick and Mary had left the children asleep, but he told the basketball boys to go on into the house and if they were somewhat quiet, they would not wake up the children. Francis said that he and the other boy went into the house; sure enough, Dick was right, the children were sleeping soundly. To the boys' surprise, neither Barry nor Evelyn woke up while they were in the house.

OTTO GUMPREHT, WANDA GUMPREHT

The Otto Gumpreht family settled just north of Toponas. They raised cattle, hay and lettuce. They had three children, Wanda, Otto "Buddy" and Janice. The icehouses for the lettuce industry were located on their property south of Finger Rock.

Wanda (Gumpreht) Redmond grew up helping on her family's ranch. After World War II, she was one of the first students from the United States to travel in the 4-H program as an IFYE delegate (International Foreign Youth Exchange) to Japan.

The Gumpreht ladies washing and rinsing clothes, circa 1900. *Courtesy of Wanda (Gumpreht) Redmond.*

HENRY HERNAGE

In 1886, Henry Hernage started a grocery store where the town of Yampa now stands.[55] Henry's first store was quite small; he carried just a few of the most basic needs in the corner of his homestead cabin. After a year or two, he was able to expand and offer more merchandise. It grew to be a large general store.

> *The Hernage store was built on the south side of what is now Moffat Avenue, across the street from the VanCamp buildings. When the early residents started mapping out the streets, they had great plans for the town. Moffat Avenue had to be one hundred feet wide so horse races and other events could be held on the street. Of course, this gave the wagons and stagecoaches plenty of room. The people of the town voted to see which side of the street would be widened. Since there were fewer people on the south side of the street, those buildings had to be moved back.[56]*

The Hernage Store on Moffat Avenue, circa 1920. *Yampa-Egeria Museum.*

By the early 1890s, Hernage's building was two stories. A few years later, the Stockman's Bank also used a section of the Hernage building. For several years, the Masons used the top floor for their lodge.

BILL HERVEY

Bill lived on Greenridge about a half mile east of where County Road 21 and Highway 131 are now. He was a good practical veterinarian and was often called to the various neighbors. He was able to treat and stich up wounds and owned a full set of tools to hold a horse's mouth open and float their teeth. Bill was called whenever a horse had trouble chewing its feed.

CARL HEROLD SR.

Carl was twelve years old when his family moved to Routt County; he was the middle child of five.[57] The hard life of a homesteader's son suited his search for adventure. His family homesteaded in Pleasant Valley, but when Carl was an adult, he had a ranch just south of what is now Stagecoach Reservoir.

Carl enjoyed music, so when he was in his late teens and early twenties, he attended many of the dances around the valley. He took his banjo with him so he could fill in if the band needed an extra player. After he grew older, one of his great loves was oil painting the surrounding land. His studies of deer and elk were very expressive.

BARNEY HODGE

Barney had an amazing mind for details, especially with machinery. He knew and remembered the numbers of most vehicle parts. When a person needed a part, he not only knew the part number but could usually find the part in his junkyard as well. One time Bill Redmond needed a part for one of his machines, so he went to Barney to see if he had that particular piece.

Barney thought for a minute and answered, "I don't have one, but I remember seeing one somewhere, let me think a minute. I know—You have one in your own junkpile, its over on the back side." Bill said that Barney had been out to his place only once and that had been two or three years before.

Another story about Barney: He was working on some electrical lines into his house, and to finish the job, he had to climb the electric pole and hook on to the main line. When he was stretching to reach the wires he needed, he inadvertently touched a live line. It knocked him off the pole, and he fell about thirty feet to the ground. He had a few burns, but the doctor told him that he was dead as he fell to the ground. It was the impact that started his heart beating again.

Barney and his wife, Helen, had two children, Nathan and Richard "Dick." I am not sure which one of them did the welding, but for a time (in the 1950s), they all drove Dodge pickups with the tailgate altered to read "Hodge."

GEORGE HOGAN

George worked for H.E. (Herb) Moore at the sawmill during the winters. George worked as an off-bearer (an off-bearer moves the newly sawn boards away from the large circular saw) on the saw and fired the boiler. His wife cooked for the men at the mill. During the summer, they lived in a house just southeast of the Yampa Cemetery.

George Hogan remarked, "Old Bill Anderson is a good sawyer, he can cut most anything from a log. He just doesn't know when he will do it."[58]

ELMER HOAG

Elmer Hoag built his homestead cabin about a half mile south of the present cemetery, on Watson Creek. In the 1880s, Elmer acted as the Egeria postmaster. The Egeria Post Office was in his cabin at that time.

Elmer Hoag hired Riley Bird to notch some logs for a barn. Riley was very good with a broadaxe and was considered by the early residents to be an outstanding log fitter. Riley notched the logs to fit while they were still lying on the ground. When the logs were lifted up for the walls, the logs did not need any more work to make the corners fit tightly. Riley worked for a while at notching the logs on the ground. He was never one to labor very long, but he made each move count. Elmer had been to town and found Riley resting when he got home. Before he even looked to see how much Riley had done, Elmer told Riley that he was paying him to notch logs, not sit around. Riley started gathering up his tools to leave; if Elmer was going to complain, he would not stay around. Evidently, it took several apologies and some fast-talking on Elmer's part to convince Riley that he really did want Riley to finish notching those logs.

JOE JOHNSON, RAWLEY JOHNSON

Joe Johnson set up a still behind his house on Greenridge where he made bootleg whiskey. A fellow named Whitley had homesteaded the place, and Joe bought it for "nothing"; he felt it was a good location to make his homebrew whiskey. This was about one mile east of the junction of the present-day County Road 21A and Highway 131.

His son, Rawley, was the same age and a good friend of Francis Moore; they enjoyed each other's company, especially during the summers. They both had horses, so the distance between their houses did not seem very great. They spent quite a bit of time fishing and hunting but also made and flew toy airplanes. Occasionally, in the winters, Rawley and Francis would ride to Wheeler Basin to ice skate on Wheeler Lake. Kids from different families around the area would meet there to skate and have a bonfire to stay warm. After Rawley left the Yampa area, he went to Denver, where he flew a plane of his own. Later he owned a gas station in Idaho Springs.

"ALCOHOL" JONES

"Alcohol" Jones got his nickname because he supposedly drank straight grain alcohol.[59] He was knowledgeable about horses. He was a practical veterinarian and able to straighten and open the cervix of an older mare that had never been bred before. Alice Laughlin had two older mares that she had tried to breed at other times. Alcohol Jones helped Francis when Francis used the stallion Silver, to breed Alice's mares. Both mares successfully had colts the next summer.

GROUSE CREEK JONES

Grouse Creek Jones lived on Grouse Creek, north of Yellow Jacket Pass. His house was about where Routt County Roads 14 and 14B intersect.

IRON SPRING JONES

Iron Spring Jones lived in a cabin near the Yampa River about four miles north of Phippsburg on County Road 14. As the name indicates, there was a mineral spring on his homestead. Some of the early settlers would stop at that spring to get water; they especially liked to make lemonade with it.

IVY KELSAY

Ivy Kelsay ran a "Fix It Shop" on Main Street in Yampa. He probably built and repaired more hay machinery than anyone else around the area. After World War II and before balers came into wide usage, he would use an old Model A Ford truck, an old Studebaker or any other old automobile and turn it into a sweep rack (also called a buck rake). He also built motorized dump rakes (sometimes called a sulky rake).

KING FAMILY

The King family (not to be confused with the Preston King family in Upper Egeria) lived on what is now County Road 21, southeast of the cemetery.[60]

Robert Laughlin sold them about ten acres for a house site. Mr. King started a strawberry patch in the small valley west of the cemetery. He did quite well with them. They were good strawberries, and he was able to trade or sell them to the grocery stores in Yampa or Oak Creek. They had a son, Ralph, who attended the school in Yampa with Francis Moore in the second and third grades.

About 1918, the King family traded land with Charlie and Nan Sanders: the King place in Routt County for the Sanders place in Arkansas. Charlie Sanders did not irrigate or weed the strawberries; consequently, they quickly stopped producing. Charlie preferred working in the timber to farming.

LAUGHLIN FAMILY

All the Laughlins worked with their hands; they made their own horse equipment, such as quirts, hackamores and so forth. Many of these items were made during the winters or in the evenings. They would sit around the kitchen table and cut rawhide thongs or "break" the rawhide strings down. (Breaking down meant that they softened the rawhide to make it more pliable and supple for braiding.) They broke down the strings by pulling them around the table legs, and this softened the fibers of the rawhide. The kitchen table had been used for this so many times that groves were worn deeply into the legs.

Even though it was not considered ladylike, the Laughlin women all rode astride and wore pants when they were camping. They usually rode astride around their own homes. Bertha did have a sidesaddle that she used when she "went to town." As she got older, she drove a light buggy to get the mail or go to the store.

BENNIE LAUGHLIN

Bennie was the second son of Robert and Francis Laughlin. He suffered with asthma most of his life and remained quite slender but was strong and wiry. Bennie loved to ride and rode as a jockey for many of the horse races around the area. He rode his own horses and for others. His own string of horses often included some of Old Nick's offspring.

In early 1903, Bennie and his wife, Percy, were the first couple to be married in the new Congregational Church (now the Yampa Bible Church).

Ben and Percy Laughlin, 1905. *Herold family collection.*

Bennie always enjoyed visiting with people; as he got older, one of his favorite pastimes was to travel from place to place and visit all his friends and relatives.

FRANCES (BIRD) LAUGHLIN

Frances was born in Missouri; she was one of thirteen children. She married Robert Laughlin there, before they came to Routt County in 1885. Three of her brothers, Olmer, Riley and Lawson Bird, also came to Routt County about that same time.

Physically, Frances was a comparatively large, robust woman. She appeared to move slowly, but each movement counted. It was said that she could fix a dinner for guests and not be rushed. A good meal would be served on time with everything in place. She enjoyed guests, especially family; most of the people from the area, if not related by actual blood, were still family to her.

When she got older, Frances would keep busy by doing needlework. In the evenings, she would sit in front of the heating stove and embroider, crochet or maybe just darn the holes in one of the grandchildren's socks. She enjoyed giving her doilies or tea towels as gifts. Whenever Frances was awake, her hands were busy.

ROBERT LAUGHLIN

After moving from Missouri to Colorado Springs, Robert Laughlin spent much time prospecting in the gold rush at Victor and Cripple Creek. He even located a couple claims in that area. One of these he named the Red Bird. Robert had no capital to develop it, so he sold it for very little. It turned out to be one of the richest mines in the area.

Robert Laughlin was very proud of his horses, especially Old Nick. The stallion Old Nick was quite fast; he won most of the races in which he was entered. Old Nick's son (Young Nick) was one of the horses to be included in the foundation horses for the Quarter Horse Association. When Young Nick was sold to Coke Roberds, his name got changed to Old Fred.

Robert Laughlin had asthma; this made him very short of breath. After he came to Egeria Park, he rode everywhere he went. When he got up in the morning, he went to the barn and saddled a horse; he then rode that horse any place he went, even if it was just back to the house so he could eat breakfast. When he got older and his joints started to stiffen, it was hard for him to climb up on a horse. He built a special stirrup for his saddle. This stirrup hung underneath and closer to the ground than the one he used when he rode. This enabled him to get into the saddle even when he was quite crippled with arthritis.

> *Robert Laughlin never swore or used foul language, but he had more pet slang expressions than anyone Francis Moore ever knew. Here are a few: glory hedgens, thunder and lightning, blue blazes, dad taked, dad burn, thunderation, tarnation, and tomfool. There may have been even more. When he got agitated, he would group two or three of them together. When he got especially irate, he would yell, "you dad-taked thing." Or "You tom fool thing." When he put them all together, "Thunderation, you dad-taked, tom fool thing!" he was really mad. He didn't seem to put the words together in any specific order.*[61]

TOM LAUGHLIN

Tom was a baby when the family came into Egeria Park. Tom was very typical for the place and time in which he grew up. He thoroughly enjoyed fishing, hunting, breaking horses and other outdoor activities. He was good at working with his hands; he braided rawhide into nosebands, quirts, reins

Ben and Tom Laughlin, 1934. *Herold family collection.*

and more. He enjoyed teaching these skills to others. When he got older, he worked with kids and taught them everything from how to rope a calf to the actual braiding of a quirt.

Tom and several other local cowboys helped Scott Teague take the author Zane Grey on a camping and hunting trip up into the Flattops. Scott Teague had a pack of hunting dogs and was known as an excellent guide for the Flattop area. Zane Grey spent several weeks fishing, hunting and just relaxing on this trip. Tom said that Grey at times appeared to enjoy sitting around the campfire and listening to the tales told by the various men.

Tom took out homestead rights on a place in Long Draw on Greenridge. Long Draw got its name from a fellow by the name of Long, not because it is physically long and narrow. This draw is southeast of Routt County Road 21A.

In the 1950s, Tom made a portable calf—it was made on a platform with wheels—so the kids could pull it across the roping arena in Oak Creek. This meant the kids could have more practice on their roping skills, and they didn't have to use live calves.

In the later part of his life, Tom drove a 1939 Chevy coup. He enjoyed both fishing and children, so he would combine his loves by loading two or three kids into his car and take them fishing. Many times, he would also take his skillet along, and lunch would be fresh fish caught during the morning.

Tom liked people and to visit with people. He would drop in on his friends, spend the afternoon talking and stay for a meal. If they had any equipment (especially saddles, bridles or harness) that needed fixing, he repaired it while he talked.

Tom relished playing with words. When one of the kids asked what something was, or what he was working on, he would often reply, "Oh, it's a whim-wham off a goose's bridle." When he replied in this manner, the kids knew that either he didn't know what something was, or more likely, they were supposed to wait and see what it was. He recognized the value of making them figure out what he was doing.

Another phrase that he used was "genuine porphyritic quartz of galena." When looking up the definitions of these words, I found that this was a "high fullootin' phrase" that meant a shiny, pretty to look at, worthless hunk of rock.

WALTER LAUGHLIN

Walter was the eldest child of Frances and Robert Laughlin. He was twelve years old when the family came to South Routt. He and his brother Ben were in charge of herding the horses and cattle on the trip from Colorado Springs; their father did ride to help them.

Even as a boy, Walter was large for his age. One day when his sisters, Bertha and Mable, were about eight and ten years old, the girls were out near the creek bank quarreling over who would do the dishes. Walter came along and said, "Stop your fighting, or I'll throw you both in the creek." With that, he grabbed both girls by an arm and swung them out over the creek. Of course, he had planned to pull them back, but the creek bank caved off and all three went into the water, which assuredly ended the quarrel.

As an adult, Walter was a large man; he stood six feet six inches tall and was quite strong. He weighed more than two hundred pounds and did not carry any extra weight. He became known around the Yampa area as a horse trainer. He was very good with horses because he didn't get angry when they disobeyed—although he would discipline an ornery horse, if he felt they needed it. He was strong enough to knock a horse down if he actually hit one.

Walter took out homestead rights to a piece of ground on Watson Creek. The buildings were on the west side of what is now Routt County Road 21. His land was just to the north of Albert Bird's homestead.

Walter and his brother-in-law Herb Moore enjoyed each other's company. They especially enjoyed hunting together for their winter's meat. Herb made the comment one time that they must have made a funny looking pair; Herb was five feet, six inches tall. Herb said that he could stand under Walter's outstretched arm.

All the Laughlins used the forge and shoed their own horses, but Walter was considered the best one at making shoes and building tools. He was a good judge of the correct temperature for forge welding the iron together.

LEM LINDSEY, T.P. LINDSEY

Moore Park Creek and Moore Park were named when Lem Lindsey and T.P. (Thomas) Lindsey came into the county and settled. When they first arrived, they called themselves Lem Moore and George Moore, thus giving the Moore name to the park where they homesteaded. When their sister Mabel (Bird) Lindsey arrived in Yampa, she informed them that they had all been born with the name Lindsey and there was no way <u>she</u> was going to use the name Moore. By the time Lem moved into town, he was using the name Lindsey. Lem Lindsey and his wife, "Auntie" Lindsey, owned the Royal Hotel for many years.

Even after the two brothers started using the name Lindsey, T.P. was called "George" more often than not.

"BILLY" (JOHN WILLIAM) MACFARLANE

As a boy, Billy Macfarlane came to Yampa with his family. As a young man, he enjoyed sports and was "quite good" at boxing.[62]

The thirteen-round bout between William Macfarlane and Young Tillman of Colorado Springs was held in Oak Creek in 1910.[63] Macfarlane lost the match by decision, but Tillman would not except a rematch in sixty days. Was Tillman afraid he would lose the $300 prize money?

Billy Macfarlane in his boxing stance, circa 1920. *Yampa-Egeria Museum, Macfarlane collection.*

Billy married Maud Laughlin and operated the M&M Garage in Yampa in the late 1920s. In a 1902 photo of Yampa, a saloon is shown on the corner of Moffat Avenue and Main Street. Billy turned the building at a forty-five-degree angle with the street. He ran a gas station there and turned the building so the gas pumps could be set in front for easy access. He and his wife, Maud, moved to Steamboat when Billy was appointed to undersheriff of Routt County in 1937.[64] Billy was elected as the Routt County sheriff in 1944 and retired from that office in 1952.

RALPH MADDOX

Ralph worked for Herb Moore at the sawmills during the winter seasons. When spring came and it was too muddy to work in a mill on Greenridge, Ralph would work around Herb's ranch, doing whatever was needed with the livestock. During the summer, he would return to his own place below Craig. Ralph was good at working with horses and enjoyed training the young colts, both the teams and the saddle horses.

Francis Moore commented, "I don't know how or when Dad [Herb Moore] first met Ralph Maddox, because Ralph's home was down on Douglas Mountain in Brown's Park."[65] In the early 1920s, Ralph came and worked for Herb in the timber several winters; he returned to Douglas Mountain in the summer.

The year Francis was sixteen and could get a hunting license, he went down to Ralph's place for hunting season. Francis stated, "There were no deer in our area at that time. Ralph took great pains to help me locate and kill my first deer. It was a real nice four-point buck."

BEN MALE

Benson "Ben" Male, the son of Dr. Jonathan Male and Edith, told the following story of the time he was sixteen and was visiting his uncle, also named Ben:

> Uncle Ben sent the young Ben out to the field for a load of hay. Ben was just at the age when he wanted to prove that he was a big strong man. He shoved the pitchfork deep into the stack to get a big forkful of hay. The handle broke. This really showed how strong he was, powerful enough to

Benson "Ben" Male and Ilda Montgomery, circa 1925. *Herold family collection.*

break the fork handle. He took the wagon back toward the house with just the few forkfuls of hay on it. Uncle Ben was not happy. He said that any dumb kid could break a handle; it took a smart man to pitch hay and not break the handle.[66]

Ben lived in the Yampa area several years. He served as youth pastor for the Yampa Congregational Church after he graduated from the Yampa High School. He then went on to a seminary to become an ordained minister and a missionary.

C.E. "ELMER" MARGERUM

Elmer enjoyed telling stories and was always good at spinning a yarn. His stories were always exciting and even seemed to get better as the years went by. Elmer enjoyed having children around. If anyone wanted to ride with him when he was making his rounds with the gas truck, he would take them along. He called both boys and girls "Oscar." We always thought this was done so he wouldn't have to remember all our names.

EDWARD H. MCCLURE

McClure bought French's blacksmith shop on Moffat Avenue just east of the VanCamp buildings. It was an old log building that had been a blacksmith shop and livery stable. McClure worked in that spot for a good many years. When he outgrew that building and needed more space, he built a new shop on his own land, just across the irrigation ditch from his house. (At the time of this writing, the house still sits on the west side of the street at First Street and Clifton Avenue.) McClure continued work as a blacksmith there until he retired and sold to Wade Davis.

> *One time when McClure was still in his shop at the Moffat Avenue location, he had a visitor come in, again, to extol his own religion. This particular fellow was a "Christian Scientist" and among other things was declaring that there was no such thing as pain, if a person would just believe in his faith. McClure had not said much, he just continued making hot rivets at the anvil. This "sales pitch" continued for some time. Finally, McClure became exasperated with the guy and picked up a red-hot rivet with his tongs, then dropped it down the man's boot top. Of course, the man jumped and hollered when he was burned. McClure just said, "If there is no pain, you can't feel that rivet." After that, the fellow no longer tried to push his religion upon McClure.*[67]

McClure had a machine that "shrank metal tires." These were the metal rims that fit around the wooden wagon wheels or the rims on the early vehicles. The machine had two clamps that would hold the metal tire and push it together so the metal became wider and thicker in that spot. He could use the machine at different spots to shrink however much was needed to make the tire fit the wooden wheel. He had to decide how much had to be shrunk out of the tire. This machine saved both time and labor, as he no longer had to cut a piece out of the metal tire and forge weld the tire back together.

GORDON MOFFATT

Gordon Moffatt had a house south of Steamboat Springs against a hillside that was east of Highway 40. In the 1960s and 1970s, it appeared to be falling down and sliding into the road but had actually been girdled by a steel cable or two and fastened to the hill. The house was certainly not straight and plumb. Gordon also owned three or four old cars, including an old Model A Ford that rattled and shimmied and looked rather unstable. Another foible was Gordon's eyes; he was rather cross-eyed. Because of these quirks, Gordon was considered to be a bit of a character by many of the people who met him.

During the 1950s and early 1960s, Gordon worked for the Hahn's Peak District of the U.S. Forest Service. When he drove a Forest Service vehicle, one of the things that he did was watch the road with one eye and scan the surrounding forest with the other eye. Gordon would describe the deer he saw on the hillside and still stay on the road. This always made his passengers, especially new employees, nervous—until they realized that Gordon's brain could process the images from both eyes at the same time.

> *One of the stories told about Gordon Moffat when he was working for the Forest Service, in the Mount Zirkel area (now a wilderness area). The trail crew was spraying for spruce beetles (the dendroxyn); Gordon sawed down a tree, when it "kicked back" and broke his leg. Larry Slate and some of the other seasonal workers were using what they called a "mule," a wheel on a ten- or twelve-foot platform to pack Gordon out. He kept telling Larry how to use the "mule" and run it around trees, rocks, etc. This "mule" was very awkward and hard to manage on a narrow rocky trail. Finally, the summer workers told Gordon that he could figure out how to get out by himself; they left him and went back up the trail. After a while, they went back to help Gordon get out to the main road where the vehicles were parked. But they told him that if he didn't keep his mouth shut, they would actually leave him to get back by himself. Evidently, he did remain somewhat quiet after that.[68]*

Gordon took outstanding photographs of wildlife and nature that were exhibited in numerous places. He had an older model German camera that had very clear optics. It was rather unusual in the fact that on a roll of film that was supposed to take thirty-six pictures, it would take almost twice that number of photos.

Gordon Moffat and Rex Gill are ready to photograph scenes on Buffalo Pass. Notice that Gordon is on skis and Rex is using snowshoes. *Courtesy of The Northwest Colorado Museum.*

Rex Gill and Gordon Moffatt were good friends; both were excellent photographers and enjoyed going into the backcountry to get their photos. Rex Gill did photography for some of the national magazines. He also painted oil pictures.[69] Rex Gill was a man who did many things well. In 1939, the *Steamboat Pilot* reported on the "house shaped like a Swiss Chalet, that Rex built behind the bath house."[70]

FRED MOHR, FLORENCE (MALE) MOHR

The Mohr family, Christian, Emelia, Ema and Fred, first arrived in Yampa during July 1912.[71] Fred was six years old; his sister was eight. Christian Mohr worked for Bill Hernage that winter, and the next year the family homesteaded at a location about eight miles west of Yampa near the Flattops. In 1917, the Mohr family left the valley for a few years. In 1925, Fred and his mother, Emelia, returned to their Yampa homestead. In 1946, Fred married Florence Male, the daughter of Dr. Jonathan Male and Edith. They bought the Royal Hotel. They rented rooms, and Florence managed the drugstore while Fred ran an upholstery business in the back of the building. They had a daughter of their own, Helen, but also adopted and raised a son, John, from Korea. They remained in Yampa for many years before they sold the Royal Hotel building in 1970; they moved to Cañon City in 1977.

MONTGOMERY FAMILY: WILLIAM MONTGOMERY, LOUISA MONTGOMERY, MERRILL MONTGOMERY

William and Louisa Montgomery started their homestead south of Yampa in the fall of 1882.[72] (Some of the family records say 1881.) Their four children helped on that small ranch. Louisa was known as a good cook, and at times, their house was a stop for the stagecoaches.

The following announcement was in the June 1905 newspaper: "Mr. Merrill Montgomery and Miss Lulu Orr were united in the holy bonds of matrimony last Sunday by Rev. Hadley. These young people are well known in this community and are much respected. The Leader joins their many friends in wishing them a prosperous and happy life."[73]

Merrill and Lulu's eldest son, Joe, bought the general store on Moffat Avenue in Yampa in the 1940s. At the time of this writing, Joe's family continues to run that establishment.

The Montgomery family. *Back*: Lulu, Ilda and Merrill; *front*: Joe, circa 1910. *Herold family collection.*

BERTHA (LAUGHLIN) MOORE

Bertha was nearly eight when she came to Routt County with her parents. On much of the trip into Egeria, she rode on the wagon seat beside her mother, who was driving one of the teams. Bertha's job was to hold the baby, Tom, on her lap and be sure he didn't fall out of the wagon. Bertha's sister Mable (age six) shared that responsibility during the trip.

Bertha enjoyed animals and, like all the Laughlins, was good at working with horses. She had been around horses since she was small and was proficient at riding and driving.

When there was no snow, people stayed on the roads, which were usually built on the ridges or along the sagebrush side hills. One reason the roads stayed on high ground was because the bottom meadows were wet and boggy in the summer. Another reason was the people tried to get the grass to grow for winter feed on the lower ground and did not want to mash it down by driving over it. Many times during the winter, people drove their sleds up through the meadows in the middle of the valley, rather than driving on the road that was a longer route. Additionally, the roads would be closed with snow drifts sooner than the open meadows were.

> One nice winter day, Bertha, Herb, and their oldest son, Earle, were going into town from the sawmill on Greenridge. At the time, Earle was just a baby, wrapped in blankets and riding on Bertha's lap. Herb was driving a pair of young horses; for some reason, they became excited and started to run. This scared Bertha because she thought that someone might get hurt if the sled tipped over.
>
> In a panic, she screamed, "Shall I throw Earle out the back?"
>
> "Don't bother." Herb replied, "The horses won't go far in this snow."
>
> However, his answer was too late; Bertha had already dropped Earle from the back of the sled. The horses quit running after a short while, then Herb and Bertha had to turn the sled to drive back to pick up Earle before they could continue their trip into town. All that excitement didn't seem to bother Earle a bit.

Francis Moore had this to say:

> My mother told me that when I was about six months old, she hooked Ben, a buckskin horse, to the little buggy, loaded me in the seat beside her and drove to Yampa—no big deal, she did it often. She had some letters to mail

and also needed to pick up the mail at the post office. Since she would only be a minute, she left horse and buggy in the street with Francis still sleeping in the seat. A small breeze picked up a piece of paper and blew it under Ben's feet, which spooked him. He took off running down the street with the buggy, baby and all. Arthur Buck, a young man known for his speed in foot races, saw the runaway coming toward him and was able to grab the horse and bring him under control. The whole episode hadn't bothered Francis. But Bertha said that Arthur sure gave her a lecture about leaving the baby without even tying the horse up.[74]

EARLE MOORE

Earle was born at the ranch of his parents, Herb and Bertha Moore. When he was six and old enough to go to school, Earle rode into Yampa each day. Earle was a very typical boy for that day and age. He enjoyed riding horses, fishing and hunting; he especially appreciated ranch life. During this time, his companions were his many cousins and uncles who lived in the area. His uncle Gordon Laughlin was just six months older than Earle, so these two became very close friends.

When Earle was in high school, he was a member of the football team. The team decided to paint their last names on the seat of their uniforms; that way, when they all bent over at the line, their last name would stand out. When Earle painted his name, the paint ran. The *Moore* turned into *Moon*. That was how Earle gained the nickname "Moon"; he continued to be called that by people in the area, even after he was out of high school and married to Virginia Godfrey.

FRANCIS MOORE

Francis was the second son of Herb and Bertha Moore. He was born in Palisade, Colorado, when his parents were there for a few months in the winter of 1909. They moved back to Routt County in the early spring of 1910. Francis spent most of the time during the first years of his life either on the ranch or at the sawmills on Greenridge. He married Gladys Margerum in 1934.

When Francis was in the first grade, he rode his horse back and forth to school. He left his horse in his grandmother Frances Laughlin's barn during

Above, left to right: Earle Moore, Virginia (Godfrey) Moore, Patsy Laughlin and Gordon Laughlin at the Bob Laughlin ranch, about 1921. *Herold family collection.*

Right: Norma, Francis and John Moore in Francis's "first Lizzy" at the H.E. Moore ranch, about 1925. *Herold family collection.*

the daytime. On his two-block walk from the school to his grandmother's house, Francis passed the town well. This was where all the kids met after school; they could combine the chore of getting water for the evening meal with the fun of playing and talking to their friends.

Francis farmed and ranched in the Yampa area the rest of his life. After he was grown, Francis was active in the community and served with many different organizations.

H.E. "HERB" MOORE

Herb Moore first came into Egeria Park about 1887. He worked for his uncle George Hughes, who was a professional guide. Instead of returning to Colorado Springs that winter, Herb stayed in Egeria Park with an old trapper, Jack Hill, near Finger Rock. Other than for various vacations, Herb spent the remainder of his life in the Yampa Valley. Herb ranched and farmed in several locations. He also owned sawmills at various sites on Greenridge.

MIKE MOSE

Mike had a place at the "edge of the quakers" about halfway between Yampa and Toponas.[75] This place is west of present-day Highway 131, on the side of Five Pine Mesa.

The first year that Francis Moore threshed for Earl Crowner, they got Mike to help. After they finished dinner, Mike pulled out a sack of Beechnut Tobacco (course cut—all purpose). He put a "big handful" in one side of his mouth, and then put a "big handful" into the other side of his mouth. As he worked, he would spend the remainder of the afternoon with both cheeks full of tobacco.

SAMUEL NAY, JOSEPHINE (BARTZ) NAY

Sam Nay married Josephine Bartz on January 16, 1907. Since Sam was delivering meat to the Moffat Railroad workers, they lived at the Gibbs ranch south of Finger Rock from April 1907 until the winter of 1908. Their first child, Norma Nay, was born on January 12, 1908, while they were still at the Gibbs ranch. They then moved to the Steamboat Springs area, where they resided for many years. Sam was well known in the Yampa area when the railroad was built, as he and his brother, Will, supplied meat to the railroad for the workers.

Sam also pitched a mean game of baseball. In 1907, his pitching helped the Yampa team win the annual Fourth of July game against the Steamboat Nine.

CHARLES NEIMAN, RUBY NEIMAN

Charley and his wife, Ruby (Carle) Neiman, owned a ranch "up the river" on what is now County Road 7. Charley was the Routt County sheriff from 1896 to 1899 and then again from 1918 to 1924. Charley's time as sheriff is probably best remembered for his capture of Harry Tracy and David Lant in Brown's Park and their recapture after they escaped from the "Bear Cage" jail in Hahn's Peak.

Ruby Neiman, daughter of Judge Carle, wrote articles for the newspapers and also recorded some of the early happenings and names of the first settlers around the Yampa area. Reference to this is found in both the *Yampa Leader* and in Dave Gray's writings.

TOM NICHOLS

The Nichols family came into the Egeria Park area at the same time as the William Bird family. Evidently, they only stayed for a very limited time, as they were gone by 1890. The Nichols name can be found on early ditch rights from the Yampa River.

H.E. Moore said that the Tom Nichols family and the William Bird family were great friends before they came to Routt County. That was why the two families built their houses very close to each other, on adjoining corners of their homestead sections. No one seems to know what happened to cause the fight between the families, but before H.E. came into the country (four years later), those two families had had a terrible fight and never did make up.

After the Nichols family moved, Jim Norvell owned the Nichols homestead property. Kenneth Hawkins bought the land in the early 1940s.

Francis Moore said that he remembered the buildings where the Nichols family lived.[76] They were falling down, and in "very bad shape" when Francis was a boy (by 1915). Francis made the comment that the Nichols boys must have been lazy carpenters, as the buildings built in the mid-1880s by other homesteaders, such as the Birds, were in fairly good shape.

Note that the buildings can be seen (in the central right meadows) in the picture of the Yampa area taken in 1909 by the Moffat Company. (A large copy of that panoramic view can be seen in the Yampa-Egeria Museum.)

JAMES "JIM" NORVELL

Jim Norvell (The Cowboy Preacher) first came into Routt County on foot, walking from Rawlins, Wyoming, to Hayden.[77] He once bragged about owning a house and living in every town in Routt County.

In Yampa Norvell was probably best known for challenging the residents to build the Congregational church. He also owned at least two ranches in Egeria Park, one in Upper Egeria at the foot of Gore Pass, the Bar O, and a ranch just north of the town of Yampa. This included the large meadows that are just north of town. The northeast area of Yampa is a plat known as the "Norvell" addition.

FRED ORR, ART ORR

George Canant hired Fred Orr to help Albert Bird run the slaughterhouse after Albert started to "get crippled up."[78] The Orrs lived at Herb Moore's place in a small newly built cabin, when Fred was working at the slaughterhouse. Art Orr was just one grade younger than Francis in school.

> *Art really enjoyed baseball and loved to pitch. Art and Francis were practicing one day on the west side of Watson Creek. Francis, using a big old catcher's mitt, was catching for Art. Francis was standing in front of the granary* [a shed with bins to store grain] *and using it for a backstop to catch any balls he might miss. Art threw a high, fast pitch— Francis did not catch it. That ball went past him and hit the boards above the log part of the granary. Francis said that yellow jacket wasps had built a nest as large as a basketball inside that wall. The boys had not seen it before they started playing catch, but the bees certainly did not like baseball. Those bees did not even ask who threw the ball! Francis was standing the closest to the wall, so the bees stung him many times. Art didn't even get stung. Francis said that he certainly remembered that day of baseball.*

OTE PERRY, MAE (BIRD) PERRY

Ote Perry was the son of W.S. and Bertha Perry. W.S. Perry bought the Bar O Ranch at the west end of Gore Pass about 1911.[79] Ote Perry homesteaded nearby and later worked as partners with his father. They ranched in the Upper Egeria Park area and raised purebred Hereford cattle for many years.

Mary "Mae" Perry was the daughter of Frank and Anna Bird. When she was in high school, she set type at the *Yampa Leader*. E.H. Godfrey owned newspaper at that time. Lettie Godfrey even helped Mae practice her graduation speech. Before she got married, Mae taught both at the school on Upper Watson Creek and the school at Pinnacle.

After Ote and Mae retired from the ranch in Toponas, they lived in a house just west of Moffat Avenue in Yampa. This was on land that Mae homesteaded in her own name. Their son "Junior" Perry operated the Toponas ranch.

JOHN PHILLIPS, LEWIS PHILLIPS

John Phillips married Betty Jane Wilson, and in the early 1880s. they came into Routt County with the Birds, Grays, Wilsons and Choates. The Phillips homestead was located just west of Finger Rock. By 1902, John Phillips operated a water-powered shingle mill at his ranch. John dropped water from the low mesa behind his house down to the mill. This artificial waterfall was enough to turn the saw for making the shingles. Phillips furnished the shingles for the new Congregational church in Yampa in 1902.

When Lewis Phillips, John and Betty Jane's son, was in high school, he and several other students played in the Yampa Town Band. After he was married, Lewis had two sons, Lawrence and Floyd. These boys were probably eight and ten years old when Francis Moore ran the threshing machine for Lewis on the mesa west of Finger Rock.[80] Someone on the threshing crew needed a short piece of binder twine. Francis looked around, couldn't find a piece and mentioned that there just wasn't any to be found. This proved to be a challenge for Floyd. He looked all around and found enough pieces to make a twine ball "bigger than a large softball."

MAURICE PIDCOCK

Maurice moved a house from a sawmill on Greenridge, and he added a second floor. The decks around both the second story and the first floor had a railing handmade from small pine poles—it was interesting and unusual architecture.

Maurice enjoyed walking and traveling, even in the middle of the winter. He would put on his snowshoes, take his rifle and a pouch of salt and be gone for several days or even a couple weeks. One of his favorite trips seemed to be to go over the top of the Flattops and into Glenwood Springs to enjoy the hot springs.

> *Even when he was older and appeared frail, Maurice carried his rifle, a 30-40 Craig, with him everywhere he went. One time when Maurice was at the Bob Laughlin place, Bob asked him if he could still hit anything with that old rifle. Maurice had rheumatism and also had trouble with his hands shaking, but when Bob questioned his shooting ability, he just walked over to a wagon, and using that wagon box for a rest, he asked Bob if he could see a small patch of snow across on the Laughlin Butte. After Bob assured him that he could see the spot, Maurice quickly fired and that small patch of snow just disappeared. Bob said that he guessed the old man could still shoot, as that was nearly a half-mile shot.*

House on Greenridge with pine pole railings built by Maurice Pidcock, photo taken in 1986. *Yampa-Egeria Museum.*

One time in the middle of the summer, when Irvin Thompson was herding sheep for Francis Moore, he heard a shot. The sound was not too far from where Irvin had the sheep, so he went to see who was shooting. Irvin found Maurice Pidcock starting to clean and field dress a young buck. Maurice appeared worried about someone finding him with that animal, so Irvin just pulled out his knife and started helping Maurice clean that deer. After they were all through, Maurice insisted that Irvin take a quarter of the meat. Irvin told him that he was just helping and didn't do it for the meat, but Maurice would not take no for an answer and maintained his position that Irvin take it. That was more than Irvin could keep from spoiling at the sheep camp, so he kept all the fresh meat he could use and then sent the rest with Francis so it would not spoil.

Even when he got older, Maurice still walked every day. He would walk from his house on Greenridge into Yampa to get the newspaper. One day, he walked the three or four miles into town, got the newspaper, walked home and sat on his porch to read it. He dozed off and never woke up. It was a little while before his wife, Louise, realized he was not just sleeping, he had passed away.

LOUISE PIDCOCK

After Maurice died, Louise Pidcock stayed on Greenridge until the girls finished the eighth grade. She then moved into town, because, as she said, "The boys'll do all right, but the girls need to go to school." There were four children: Frank, Bill, Marguerite and Evelyn. The Pidcock family lived just one block from the school in Yampa. They brought their milk cow with them from their Greenridge ranch, and each morning, one of them would lead the cow out of town and tether her in a spot along the railroad tracks so she could graze during the day.

Louise Pidcock also liked to walk; neither she nor the girls would ride when they could walk. When she

Maurice and Louise Pidcock with baby Margaret, about 1912. *Yampa-Egeria Museum.*

was in her late seventies or early eighties, she and her daughters decided to walk to Trappers Lake and back, a trip of fifty miles. This was a one-day trip that they had evidently made many times. When she got back, Mrs. Pidcock made the statement, "I just can't do it anymore. I had to sit and rest while the girls made side trips."

FRANK PIDCOCK

When Frank Pidcock (son of Maurice and Louise) was in his late teens, he worked for Francis Moore putting up hay. This was in the long meadow that Kenneth Hawkins owned at the time. Francis said that Frank was strong, especially in his hands and fingers, and very athletic. When they came in for lunch, he would back up to the side of the house, then reach up to the eaves of the house, grip the edge with his fingers and swing up onto the roof in a backward summersault-type movement.

ARNOLD POWELL

Arnold Powell and his wife came from England. He was one of the owners and the president of the Yampa Bank when the bank had to close in the early 1930s. They also owned a cattle ranch about two miles west of Yampa on what is now County Road 17.

JAMES REDMOND, JACK REDMOND

From 1910 through 1920, many different people homesteaded on the land west of Yampa. The Redmond family settled on South Hunt Creek. This is one of the few early settlers whose family still remains in the area.

In the 1920s, the settlers made an early attempt to start an irrigation reservoir in Allen Basin; however, the cost of development was prohibitive, and nothing was done at that time.[81]

In 1956, James's son, James T. "Jack," was a shareholder for the construction of a reservoir.[82] Jack was the secretary for the corporation and was instrumental in obtaining the name *Allen Basin Reservoir* for the group.

Arnold Powell's ranch house about two miles west of Yampa, Colorado, circa 1920. *Herold family collection.*

Jack and Wanda Redmond's house west of Yampa. The yard light is one of the original street lights from Moffat Avenue in Yampa. *Herold family collection.*

"JACK RABBIT JIMMY" FRANK WRIGHT:

"Jack Rabbit Jimmy" homesteaded a small piece of land on the flats west of Yampa, right next to Watson Creek at a bend in the road.[83] (It was about six miles west of Yampa on what is now County Road 11.) Legend said he received his nickname because all that he and his family had to eat one winter was jackrabbits. After the Powells moved to California, the Wright family lived at Arnold Powell's place. Later, he moved his family to the Hoag homestead on what is now County Road 21. Frank had a son, Gene, who was big and husky, but had the mind of a six- or seven-year-old. Gene helped Arnold Powell during haying. Powell could not dump the rake; it was too hard to push the lever. Gene asked to try to dump it. He dumped it easily, but after he found that he could, he would not do it again.

"MOP STICK" WRIGHT

"Mop Stick" received his name because he traveled from town to town and went from door to door selling mop sticks.[84] This was a special mop with a crank to wring out the excess water. He lived on a small place northwest of Yampa.

RUBE SQUIRE

Rube Squire was born in Hayden, Colorado, in 1892 and worked as a cowboy throughout much of Routt County.[85] He was also a carpenter and general handyman, as he worked on several of the homes around the Yampa area, adding on rooms or even building the houses. His trademark was to set the logs perpendicular to the ground to make the exterior of the house. Rube loved bucking horses and could remember who rode which horse in the various contests. Francis Moore commented, "Rube had an excellent memory for both names and dates."[86] When Rube got older, he had an extensive collection of photographs of the many different horses he remembered. Rube also wrote several articles for magazines, including the *Western Horseman*, about the early horses and riders from the Western Colorado area.

Rube Squire riding his horse, Monday, in a Stake Race at a Steamboat Springs rodeo, 1919. *Yampa-Egeria Museum.*

CHARLES "CHUCK" STARK

Chuck was the Yampa town marshal for a while (probably in the late 1920s).[87] Barney and Helen Hodge got married, and as was the custom, the young people of the town gave them a *shivaree.* (Newlyweds could expect their friends stop by some night to "serenade" them by beating on pots and pans and blowing horns. It would turn into a party with refreshments and at times even a dance.) Chuck threw Barney into the Yampa jail as part of the shivaree celebration —of course everyone thought that was extremely funny. Chuck let him out the next morning. Later, Chuck went to Denver and worked in an auto body shop, straightening out old cars.

LAWRENCE STARK

Lawrence homesteaded the top of the Devils Grave Mesa (west of Yampa), 1,200 acres. He burned the brush off and then planted it into grain and grass. It made productive fields, growing oats and wheat. Everyone else had assumed it was worthless land and did not realize that it could be a valuable dryland farm.

SCOTT TEAGUE

Scott was a well-known hunter and guide into the Flattops, the Hahn's Peak, Mount Zirkel and California Park areas. He was the guide and outfitter for both Teddy Roosevelt and Zane Grey when they visited the Flattops. Both the *Steamboat Pilot* and the *Yampa Leader* published articles about his exploits. When he was not hunting, he kept his hounds behind his house on Moffat Avenue. When it was their feeding time, the baying of those dogs could be heard all over the valley.

> *If it was a large or prestigious group to be taken into the mountains, Scott would hire some of the local cowboys as horse wranglers and camp cooks. When Scott took Zane Grey into the Flattops, they had a horse herd of seventy or eighty animals. Vern Caldwell and Virgil Marshall were the head wranglers but had the help of several other local cowboys. None of the local cowboys, including Tom Laughlin, Gordon Laughlin, Bob Laughlin and "Doc" Marshal, were impressed with Zane Grey. They said he would sit for hours and do nothing but stare at a flower or a tree leaf. But evidently Grey was not impressed with the cowboys either, as he called them "uncouth."* [88]

Oren Gray and Scott Teague holding a lynx. *Historical Society of Oak Creek and Phippsburg, Riggin Collection.*

LEVI TRANTHAM, CAREY TRANTHAM, MYRTIE (BIRD) TRANTHAM

Levi came to Yampa in the early 1900s. He had a real estate office on Moffat Avenue and soon started teaching at the high school. One of his students was Myrtie Bird. According to the stories, when school was out for the summer, Levi got on the train to leave the area. Myrtie jumped on the train right behind him and told him, "If you are leaving, I'm going along." They rode the train as far as Toponas before coming back to Yampa to get married. They remained in the Yampa area for the rest of their lives. Levi and Myrtie had two children, Carey and Ione.

Myrtie used a large kettle in the yard to make her own lye soap even after she was older and soap was readily available in stores. She felt her own soap did a better job getting everything clean. A bar was always on the washstand to scrub dirty children's and adults; hands. Clothes were washed in shavings of that lye soap.

Myrtie enjoyed children, especially her grandchildren and any of their friends they brought with them. She encouraged their imaginations and didn't mind a little mud after they made mud pies.

Levi had a wonderful bass voice, and until he became quite deaf, his voice always added a wonderful resonance to the church hymns. Levi Trantham was already getting deaf by the time his son was ten or so. Levi and his father-in-law, Albert Bird, used an overshot stacker. This type of stacker used a basket to hold the hay as it was being sent to the top of the stack. This overshot stacker built a smaller stack than the plunger-type stackers.

One haying season, Levi was on top of the stack, doing the job of a stack builder. Carey was ten or eleven years old and just learning how to run the team for putting the basket of hay up onto the stack. Carey had found that he could be a "smart aleck" and say things quietly that Levi could not hear. This particular day, Levi told Carey to push the hay up with an easy shove so it would fall close to the stacker. In a quiet voice, as he had been doing, Carey called his father "a god-dammed, stupid old man." The sound waves were just right for Levi, who was directly above Carey, to hear this bit of insolent cursing. Immediately, Levi slid off the stack and grabbed Carey, giving him a well-deserved licking. A fellow by the name of "Alcohol" Jones was working for Levi at the time as a sweep rake driver. He was the one who later related the incident to Francis Moore.[89]

Levi and Myrtie lived in the frame house that Myrtie's father, Albert Bird, built about 1900. When they got older, they sold the place and moved into a small house on Main Street in Yampa. Even then Myrtie maintained a large garden and could be seen pulling weeds while wearing her old calico sunbonnet.

I.J. "IRA" VANCAMP

Most likely, the VanCamp family came into Yampa in the fall of 1884.[90] The cattle rustler Joe Ward had just been told to leave the area. The VanCamps then moved into the house that Ward had acquired the summer before. This area with the large cottonwood trees soon became known as the VanCamp Grove. The VanCamps operated a stage stop and roadhouse for several years, until the Antlers Hotel was built. The family also owned other enterprises, a family ranch, the stage line to Dunkley and a drugstore. The VanCamps became well known for their hospitality and their service to the community. Ira was a town trustee at times and also served a couple terms as the mayor of Yampa.[91]

An article from the *Yampa Leader* in 1905 proclaimed,

> *I.J. VanCamp has sold his drug store on Moffat Avenue to Mr. Goodwin of New Castle, the optician who was advertised to be at the Antlers last Monday. Mr. Goodwin is a registered pharmacist and graduate optician. He left Sunday for New Castle to arrange his business affairs and with his family expects to return here in a few days to remain permanently.[92]*

E.H. "ED" WATSON

Ed Watson came into South Routt in 1881. He built a small cabin just east of the present Yampa Cemetery. (Robert Laughlin bought this homestead from a second party in 1885.) Ed Watson lived at this location for two or three years. Ed Watson stayed in Egeria Park that first winter with his wife.[93] Thus, Mrs. Watson was the first Caucasian woman to spend the winter in Egeria Park. The first election in Egeria Park was held in the cabin of E.H. Watson. Since most of the settlers went back to their families that fall, very few people were left in the area to vote. The judges and clerks could vote of course, but most of the voters were on the election board. "The Judges and Clerks for this election were Ed Watson, L.L. Wilson, James Scott, Sam Fix and Peter Simon. The voter was Doc Baxter from Sunnyside."[94]

The first Egeria Park post office was at the Watson ranch in 1883, with E.H. Watson acting as the first postmaster. The creek that ran through his ranch still bears the name Watson Creek.

DON WILMER "BILLY" WHIPPLE, J.W. WHIPPLE

Don Wilmer "Billy" Whipple wrote to the *Steamboat Pilot* with the following information. "In the winter of 1879 there were several of us who wintered in Egeria up until Christmas and then moved to Rock Creek for the balance of the winter."[95]

Billy and his brother J.W. Whipple started the first stagecoach line from Wolcott to Yampa and Steamboat. Billy was a stagecoach driver much of the time. J.W. homesteaded just southeast of the present location of Phippsburg. Whipple Creek carries his name.

"CURLY" WILLIAMS, ELSIE WILLIAMS CERISE

One year (probably in the early 1930s), Francis Moore was driving an old caterpillar tractor in the lane above Yampa, when "Curly" Williams drove past him.[96] Francis went a few hundred yards farther and found a tie-rod lying in the middle of the road. Francis stopped and picked it up. Curly went on up the road, visited with a neighbor for a few minutes and came back. Francis stopped him and asked if it was his tie-rod. Curly shook his head and said he didn't think so but jumped out to see if it had fallen off his old truck. It had! Curly had turned completely around in the neighbor's yard and had not even noticed that only one wheel was doing the turning.

Curly's wife was Elsie, and they had two boys, Jack and Paul. Several years after Curly died, Elsie married a man with the last name Cerise. Elsie was one of the first cooks for the hot lunch program at the Yampa School in the early 1950s.

THE STORIES OF DIFFERENT people are what bring history to life. Tidbits add insight however small; the uniqueness of the characters and their environment are in some cases all that are left. Today, what remains is the area, the archived pieces, the people who live here now and the stories that have yet to be preserved for future generations.

4

HORSES, BEAR AND OTHER ANIMALS

A nimals have always been an integral part of life in all cultures. It was certainly no different for those early settlers in Routt County. Because people were dependent on animals, those same animals became the center of many stories and legends.

Horses were essential to the first settlers who came into the area, as most of the early travel was done on horseback. Moving wagons over game trails and horse paths was slow if not impossible. Extensive wagon travel was not attempted until the roads improved. Wagons then brought household goods and tools for establishing homes. In the Yampa Valley, donkeys and mules were mostly used as pack animals, rather than used to ride or as heavy draft animals. There were almost no oxen used as draft animals in Routt County. The stage lines from both Middle Park and Wolcott utilized horses. In the winter, people sometimes used skis or snowshoes as a means of transportation. However, prior to the railroad arriving in 1908, the horse was supreme.

Many ranches raised horses as part of their ranching activities. Draft horses could vary greatly in size and stature. Some of them were almost the size of a saddle horse, 900 to 1,200 pounds; people often drove those on their buggies and wagons when they went to town, as they could usually travel faster than the heavier horses that were bred for strength. The heaviest draft horses were used in the fields to plow and harrow the grain and hay crops. The timbermen seemed to like middle-size horses for skid horses; most of those ranged from 1,100 to 1,500 pounds.

Unidentified man leaving for a camping trip at the John Phillips ranch. Finger Rock is in the background. *Herold family collection.*

These homesteaders are picking up shocks of grain so the grain can be stacked, circa 1905. *Herold family collection.*

Saddle horses were used in contests, horse races, stake races, roping and bucking. But the ranchers and farmers also held contests with their draft horses. Many times, those same horses were also used in the everyday work of cutting and stacking hay or planting and harvesting grain.

Those early ranchers did not particularly breed to raise bucking horses, but if they had a horse that was good at bucking, they would take it to the different rodeos around the valley. It was an honor to have one's horse designated as the "worst horse."

Because horses were so important, everyone had a favorite horse or two and countless stories to tell.

"Old" Nick was an important part of "Granddad" Robert Laughlin's life. He was truly a horse from which legends were made. Evidently, Nick was young (possibly a yearling or two-year-old colt) when the family first left Missouri. By the time Robert got to Sedalia and Colorado Springs, he could make enough money to buy groceries for the family by racing Nick. Part of the time, Robert would ride the horse himself, but most of the time he would have his son Bennie ride Nick. Bennie did not weigh very much, so that gave a greater advantage to Nick in his races. By the time the Laughlins came into Routt County, some of the animals in the family horse herd were sired by Nick. Robert bred and raised many horses, but like so many things tried in the area, "the bottom fell out of the market" so he didn't get rich. Robert rode Nick as a saddle horse wherever he went even though he was a stallion.

> One time when Robert Laughlin arrived in Hayden, a horse race was just beginning. Knowing that Nick was fast, everyone shouted at Robert to join in the race. Robert did, even though he was riding a heavy stock saddle and had his saddlebags full of staples and other fencing supplies behind the saddle. The starter lined the horses up and shouted go. Robert just sat there. "Go, man, go!" shouted the starter again.
>
> "I thought you said ho," replied Robert over his shoulder as he kicked Nick into a run. In spite of the heavy weight and the late start, Nick won the race.[97]

Bertha (Laughlin) Moore said that Nick was the most active horse she had ever seen.[98] Old Nick would be alone in the corral, and just for exercise he would raise his front feet off the ground and take several steps with just his hind feet, an amazing performance.

Nick won numerous races in his lifetime and sired many protégé. Some of his offspring were quite fast; most were dependable saddle or wagon horses.

Robert Laughlin holding
Old Nick, circa 1880.
Herold family collection.

Robert Laughlin kept a son of Old Nick; inevitably, this horse became "Young" Nick . Young Nick was as fast as his sire had been; he too became an important part of the Laughlin horse herds. The offspring were used as working cattle horses, racehorses and buggy horses. Bennie Laughlin made the comment one time, "They had common sense."

In 1947, *Westerner Magazine* talked about quarter horses and how they had been started in Routt County by Coke Roberds of Hayden, who had a horse called "Old" Fred. That magazine did not give the early history of Old Fred.

According to Mae Perry in a follow-up letter to the *Record Stockman* (the sponsoring publication for the *Westerner*), a man by the name of John Stockton of Dade County, Missouri, went back to Tennessee and purchased a sire called "Little Nick." (That was the sire of Robert Laughlin's "Nick.") Robert acquired his Nick from John Stockton.

Family legend has several men traveling to Tennessee at the close of the Civil War and stealing a small horse herd to keep those horses out of the soldiers' hands. Those horses included the Nick line. Ben Laughlin, Robert's son, sold Young Nick to Coke Roberds. Roberds then changed the horse's name to Fred.

In July 1916, the Hayden newspaper had this to say: "Coke Roberds brot in [from Yampa] a famous race horse stallion this week and will use it for breeding purposes."[99]

The names Nick, Little Nick, Old Nick, Young Nick and Fred all seem to be mixed together according to who told the stories. There is strong evidence, when following the historical dates and the stories told by the residents at the time, that Young Nick and Fred were the same horse, first bred and raised by Robert Laughlin then sold to Coke Roberds by Robert Laughlin's son, Ben.

Herb Moore told the following story:

> *Shortly after Herb and Bertha were married, they were on their way to Yampa, driving a light active team hooked to a small buggy so they were trotting right along. They caught up to "Grandpa" Bill Bird, who was driving a heavy work team hooked to a full-sized wagon with dump boards, at a slow plodding walk. Sitting behind their father on two kitchen chairs were the two youngest boys of the family, Frank and Loren. Herb didn't want to follow behind at a slow walk, so thought he would pass by and go on, but as he started to go by, Bill grabbed his whip and yelled "Hi-Ya." He struck both horses with the whip, the team lunged forward and both boys, together with their kitchen chairs, tumbled off the back of the wagon.*
>
> *Herb shouted to Bill, "You lost your passengers!"*
>
> *Bill misunderstood and called back, "You won't pass me," as he kept whipping for more speed. When Bill finally realized what had happened, the boys were about a quarter of a mile back down the road coming along carrying their chairs. Herb said he found out later that many old-time Missourians considered it a disgrace to be passed by anyone at any time.*[100]

Herb Moore talked about the difference in sizes of the saddle horses in the 1800s when he came into Egeria Park. Herb had traveled from East Texas to the XIT Ranch, where he worked as a horse wrangler. The horses in Texas were fairly small, running thirteen to fourteen hands in height. The horses in the Egeria Park area were much larger; those horses with their Missouri influence averaged fifteen to sixteen hands tall.

In those days, horses were trained differently. Young colts were broken to lead. After they were weaned, they would be turned out and not schooled any further until they were at least three years old; many times they would be four or five years old. The horse owners and trainers of that time wanted the animals to have their growth and have their bones fully developed before they were trained to harness or the saddle.

As she got older, Bertha (Laughlin) Moore drove a light buggy more than she rode, especially if she were going into town to visit or get the mail.[101] Her buggy had a small cloth top, and the front wheels were slightly smaller than the back wheels. It had a small step (Francis Moore held his hands out and pictured about an eight-inch oval) so one could easily get up into the buggy, even with a skirt. One of Bertha's favorite horses was Old Ben, a large, gentle horse that Herb Moore had gotten from Carl LaBounty. Ben could be either driven or ridden; Carl LaBounty said he was used as a stagecoach horse before the Moores bought him.

RALPH MADDOX HAD A place on Douglas Mountain in Brown's Park. He spent the winters in the Yampa area during the late 1910s and early 1920s. He would work for H.E. Moore in the timber until "spring break-up" then he would work on H.E.'s ranch for a month or so before going back to Douglas Mountain. Ralph Maddox was very good at breaking horses, especially riding horses.[102]

Francis Moore remembered one time that Ralph broke a little buckskin mare they called Bossy. Ralph had only ridden her once before, when a bull got into their neighbor's cattle.

> *When I got home from school, Ralph was sitting on the ground leaning against the gate post, with Bossy and the bull roped together. He couldn't get the rope off alone so was waiting for my help. Ralph was laughing at the little green-broke mare, the bull would try to go somewhere and catch Bossy sidewise and almost jerk her down until she found she could hold that bull if she turned toward him.*

The neighbor, Lon Wilson, said when Ralph came to check after the bull, he saw that Ralph was riding a horse not even bridle-wise, so he told Ralph if he would wait until he (Lon) got his hay unloaded he would help him.

But, Ralph replied, "Oh, no, I didn't come to see how he was doing, I came to get him." With that, Ralph lassoed the bull and started hazing him toward home. That was Ralph's method: teach a newly broke horse everything he expected him to know right from the beginning.

CECIL CONNER SPENT THE early part of his life in the Maybell and Brown's Park area, riding for the area ranchers and also catching and training horses from the wild herds. He was the oldest child and was raised on a homestead west of Maybell. In the mid-1950s, he came to South Routt County and lived on a Greenridge ranch. Later, he and his wife, Helen, moved into the town of Phippsburg. He was well known for both his horsehair hitching and rawhide braiding on hackamores and other horse equipment.

Cecil Conner said that when he was down in the Maybell area he caught (from the wild herds in Brown's Park) and broke many different horses to ride. The worst horse he ever tried to work with was a gray. This horse was "really nice looking," but even after Cecil had tried many times to ride and break him, he still reared over backward if he could not unseat his rider any other way. Cecil said that at that time they did not think anyone should have to "snub" a horse to another horse's saddle horn to train him to work as a cow horse. This gray was so bad that they even tried the "snubbing" to get him over his rearing up and falling over backward. They turned that horse loose for a while and got him in later and tried again; they still did not have any luck in stopping the horse from rearing. Again, they tried everything they could think of, including "snubbing" him to another horse's saddle horn. It still did not work. Every time they tried to ride him by himself, he would rear over backward. Finally, they turned him back out on the range with their loose horses, because they were afraid that someone was going to get hurt. A rancher from Utah came through, picking up some of his own stock from the area. This fellow was known for taking not only his own animals but also any others that he could steal. Cecil said during different years people from the Browns Park area had to go into Utah to get their own stock

Cecil Connor is repairing the corral at his Greenridge ranch, 1985. *Herold family collection.*

*back from this fellow. This time when the Utah horse rancher picked up his
own horses, he also took the gray horse. Cecil said that he did not even try to
get that horse back; he thought that man and horse deserved each other. Cecil
said that he never heard of any kid getting killed or crippled from a gray
horse, so the fellow must not have put any kids up on him.*[103]

Cecil's favorite horse was a big rawboned horse named Blackie.[104] Cecil
said he still got "choked up" when he thought about that horse. One time,
an easterner brought in a "fancy thoroughbred" so he could help chase
and catch the wild horses. Rather than try to chase the horses into pens
or corrals, they were just going to have their friends chase the horses for
a while until they tired, then the easterner was going to catch the one he
wanted with a rope. Cecil said that they chased and chased that wild horse,
with the easterner remaining about two rope lengths behind. That fancy
eastern horse just could not catch the wild one. The wild horse was about
to go up and over a saddle into an area that the riders could not follow.
The tenderfoot's thoroughbred was too tired to go any faster. Cecil kicked
Blackie and was able to get close enough to catch that wild horse before it
disappeared down the slick rock hillside. Cecil said he was "real proud of
Blackie that day."

CATCHING WILD HORSES IN different areas required site-specific strategies.
When the Marshall brothers went to Moffat County to get horses, this was
the story that was told:

Not long after World War I, Doc (Lawrence) Marshall and his brother
Virgil went to Wolf Creek, about forty-five miles west of Meeker. Doc recalled
using a relay system when chasing the wild horses. They must have been quite
successful using this method in the Meeker area, as they caught sixty head of
horses and picked out the best ones. They turned the rest loose. [105]

When the Marshall brothers traveled to the Meeker area, they used Vern
Caldwell's corrals to contain the wild horses until they were ready to trail
them back over the Flattops to Yampa.[106] Vern had a cabin west of Meeker
where he did some trapping. Vern Caldwell and Virgil Marshall were good
friends and enjoyed spending time together.

A story that "Doc" told:

*He and his brother Dewy had some really fast saddle horses. They thought
if they took them down to Brown's Park they could easily round up those*

Moffat Avenue in Yampa was the starting point for Virgil and "Doc" Marshall to look for wild horses near Meeker, 1921. *Courtesy of Linda Long.*

> *wild horses. They soon found their fast grain-fed horses were not a match for those wild mustangs in their native surroundings. Doc said they couldn't keep near enough to those wild horses to even see which way they had gone and soon lost them.*[107]

Ralph Maddox, a Brown's Park cowboy, said the Marshalls went at it in the wrong way; it was impossible in that rough canyon country to outrun the wild horses. At that time, the people in the Brown's Park area depended on the wild horses for their living.

The way Ralph and his neighbors caught them was to just walk them down, day after day. The first day, Ralph said a rider could barely get close enough to see them disappear over a distant ridge, but by staying with it, and never letting those wild ones stop for feed or water, the second day a cowboy could get a little closer. By the third day of relentless moving, with no water, one could possibly get near enough to begin directing them toward a trap that was prepared in a canyon or someplace to bottle them up. Ralph and his neighbors seemed to know how, because all the horses they rode came from that wild bunch. Ralph told of one extremely smart old mare that could sense or smell a trap a mile away. She would gather her colt and maybe two or three others, break out of the group and stampede for the hills. When that happened, they were extremely lucky if they didn't lose the whole bunch. After that old mare had pulled that stunt two or three times, Ralph said, "We finally shot her; that was the only way to stop her from breaking away and taking others with her."

This ad was in the 1910 *Yampa Leader* newspaper:

Registered Percheron Horses.

Hunick Bros. have three young thoroughbred Percheron stallions at the ranch of J.R. Powell, five miles west of Yampa, the finest horses ever brought to Routt County. Arrangements may now be made for service during the coming season, or for the purchase of either of the horses. Pedigrees may be seen at Leader office.[108]

Francis Moore's uncle Cecil Long (Theresa Laughlin's husband) worked for Herb Moore on and off for many years.[109] Cecil loved horses, especially good pulling horses. About the first team of Herb's that Cecil drove was Jeff and Chub. As a team, they were not well matched; they were not the same size or the same color. Jeff was jet black except for a small white streak down his face; Chub was a gray roan. Jeff was a fast, spirited walker, while Chub

Percheron team north of Yampa, circa 1990. *Herold family collection.*

always had to be prodded to keep up. However, they were matched in their ability to pull. They would both just get down and "scratch" until something gave. That is what Cecil really loved about them.

Because of their mismatch in speed, Herb split them up and teamed Jeff with a black, fast, spirited walker, which Herb needed in a road team. They matched Chub with his half sister, also a gray roan and gaited more to his slow plodding speed; her name was Pet. With practically all the lumber, tie and prop sales in Oak Creek and beyond, Herb favored the fast-walking teams.

RUBE SQUIRE WAS A well-known cowboy and acted as a judge for some of the bucking horse contests and other horse events around the entire Yampa Valley. He listed some of the riders and some of the famous horses that came from the Egeria Park area.[110] The following were top bronc riders: O.L. Grimsley, Emory Clark, Ivan Decker, Lawrence Marshall, George Bird, Jim Wilson, Texas Evans, Art Orr, Jesse Adams, Walter Laughlin, Lowell Wilson, Jim Fulton and George Eller.

Egeria Park also produced many top bucking horses. These included King Mountain and Gravel Gertie, owned by Hank Fox; Cork Screw, owned by Doc (Lawrence) Marshall; Hired Girl, owned by George Bird; Cactus Kate, owned by Virgil Marshall; Blue Dog, owned by Mart Pitts; Gray Eagle, owned by Bruce Roup; Brown Joe, owned by Charlie Whitely; Ten High, owned by Jim Wilson; Shimmy Shaker, owned by Evart Wilson; Dynamite, owned by George Crawford; General Pershing, owned by Frank Squire; Skylark, owned by Andy Squire. Prohibition, owned by Al Paggett; and Pin Ears and Carrie Nation, owned by Lou Long.

The list of good bucking horses and their owners is interesting because the owners list also includes many of those listed as the best riders.

One of the more talked-about horses was Pin Ears. He made a name for himself from 1903 until at least 1910. Rube Squire told the following stories:

On Labor Day, 1910, at Oak Creek John Brenton had a go round with Pin Ears. He made a good try, but couldn't stay aboard. He landed on his feet close behind the horse and gave him one more rap with the quirt for good measure. As Lou Long, the owner walked out to catch the horse, he extended his hand. Pin Ears, the outlaw, picked up with his forefoot and shook hands with him. Pin Ears was a smart horse and not the mankiller some folks have pictured him to have been. I've seen him in action many times, and never did he try to harm the rider who was bucked off.

Rodeo on Airport Hill west of Yampa. Notice that the judges are on foot, circa 1920. *Yampa-Egeria Museum.*

In 1920, Edgar Bobbitt…His ride on General Pershing was one of the outstanding rides of all time. After several jumps Pershing landed standing straight up on his hind feet, came within an ace of going over backward, and from there on used the antics of a kangaroo, never putting his forefeet to the ground. He would go in the air like a skyrocket, always land on his hind feet, then double up like a jackknife, with a terrific come back. Just how that young cowboy ever stayed aboard, I'll never know.[111]

George Bird was considered to be one of the "prettiest" riders in the area. He was a good rider and much of the time he wore a fancy pair of white hair-on chaps. He didn't always ride his horse, but when he did, it always looked good to both the judges and to the audience.[112] At different times, he rode in most of the rodeos in northwest Colorado as well as at the Cheyenne Frontier Days in Wyoming. One of the stories told about the Birds was that when they were young (six or eight years old), they had a donkey that was ornery and would buck. The brothers would dare each other to ride that donkey. Supposedly, that was how George learned to be such a good rider.

On the Fourth of July at Steamboat Springs, 1924, Toughy Wren took first, Stanley Larson, second.[113] Tiger Tom was awarded bad horse money. With the men drawing to see who would ride Pershing, George Bird was the lucky guy. He managed to ride him, too, which brought much applause from the large crowd.

During the 1920s, General Pershing was probably one of the finest bucking horses anywhere in the area. Many horses have a set pattern in the way they will buck. A good rider can anticipate what the horse's next move will be. General Pershing did not have any pattern to his moves; he might do some straight bucking with deep dives, then stand on his back legs so he felt like he would rear over backward. The next time, he might buck and sunfish to the left or to the right. In the rodeos of today, a horse is never ridden more than once a day and many times only once or twice a week. In the 1920s, it was not unusual for one of the good bucking horses to be ridden several times during a single rodeo. Those horses were truly great athletes.

> *General Pershing was owned and raised by Rube and Frank Squire in Yampa. They started to train him to be a saddle horse. Rube had ridden him several times and was treating him as an ordinary saddle horse. He got part way to Toponas and dismounted for some reason. When he started to get back on, Pershing started to buck and bucked him off. He tried to mount again, once more Rube hit the ground. The next time, Rube tied Pershing solid to a pole as he tried to mount. Pershing still bucked and threw him off. That was the last time anyone tried to use General Pershing as an ordinary saddle horse.*[114]

Bear stories have been a part of life for as long as humans have been recording handed-down tales. Bears have been both revered and hunted by the Native Americans as well as the people of all nations around the world. There were many bears in Egeria Park when the first permanent settlers came to the valley; even the Yampa River was then called the Bear River. The Utes that summered in what is now Routt County told of the bears eating the yampa roots. In June 1874, James Crawford observed, "Bear seemed to be everywhere—black, cinnamon, and grizzly," as he went down the valley toward Steamboat Springs.[115]

In 1887 when H.E. Moore first came into South Routt, he was with his uncle George Hughes. George was a guide for hunters that came from Denver or "back east." The place that Hughes liked to hunt the best was up in the Flattop area. This is the way H.E. told the story:

> *We saw the huge tracks of a grizzly bear. They were the size of the bottom end of a large ham.* [He would hold up his hands to show an oval about fourteen or sixteen inches in length.] *We tracked that bear and finally caught up with him in a small park. George shot the bear, but it*

Above: Many rodeos and horse events have been held on Moffat Avenue in Yampa, circa 1910. *Yampa-Egeria Museum.*

Left: Proud bear hunters with their bear, circa 1920. *Herold family collection.*

did not drop. It started roaring and lumbering toward us. It was throwing a fit as if it could not see anything. It grabbed a small "quaker" [quaking aspen] tree as big around as my wrist and jerked it out of the ground. All the while, it was roaring and coming toward us. I raised my rifle to shoot that bear a second time.

Uncle George knocked up my gun and said, "Don't shoot, he's already dead." The bear roared and came even closer. He did finally fall over and die a few yards in front of us, but he tore up quite a bit of ground and trees before he actually died.

After it was all over, Herb told Uncle George, "Don't you ever knock my gun aside again!" Herb said he could literally feel the hair on the back of his neck starting to fall back into place. It had "stood straight up" while the bear was charging them.

Bears were still having an effect on the valley in the 1900s. The *Yampa Leader* offered a story with the headline "Big Bear Hunt in Routt County—Bears Killing Stock."[116] The article continued to say that at least one hundred young horses had been killed by bear that spring. The bears were hungry and dangerous because of both the high number of bears and the long winter hibernation. Albert Whitney and Steve Elkins would have a pack of forty hounds to take the Denver hunters on the spring bear hunt. That hunt was scheduled to start on May 5, 1909.

The homesteaders fenced much of the area around their houses in Egeria Park. The fences that most people built were to keep animals out of their grain fields or out of the meadows that had to be cut and saved for winter feed. The areas used for pasture were considered open range. Some of the open range was deeded land that had not been fenced, but most of it was government land. The various ranchers hired a range rider to look after the stock during the summers.

In one of his manuscripts, Francis Moore mentioned that there weren't any bear stories in all his reminiscing, so it was time for a couple.[117] Francis didn't know the year, but Lowell Wilson was range rider for the group ranging cattle on upper Morrison Creek:

Lowell Wilson said he had heard of people roping bear all of his life so he thought if the opportunity ever comes; "I am going to try it." This particular day, he was riding a little iron-gray mare of Bob Laughlin's, when he sighted a pretty good-sized, black bear. So, Lowell thought, "here's my chance," as he built a loop, spurred for the bear and caught it—first

Scott Teague and his pack of hounds with a treed bear, circa 1920. *Yampa-Egeria Museum.*

throw! He said the rope had barely tightened on the bear's neck when that bear wheeled and came right back up the rope at him.

Lowell said, "The horse was quicker than I was in turning and getting out of there," even so, the bear made a big leap and struck out with a front paw which left four gashes from its claws down the little mare's rump. In the mad rush that followed, the bear went on one side of a tree and Lowell and the horse on the other side, thus breaking the rope. Lowell said that was the only time he was ever happy to see a rope break. By the time he brought the horse under control, the bear was nowhere in sight, for which Lowell was very thankful. The wounds from those claws were not very deep so they soon healed, but being an iron-gray color, the hair in those scars grew in black. So, the little mare had four black streaks down her hip for the rest of her life. Furthermore, Francis was sure that Lowell never roped any more bears the rest of his life.

About 1950, there was apparently one bear that made the rounds of three sheep herds.[118] Maneotis's on Morrison Creek, Hamilton's in Wheeler Basin and Moore's on Greenridge. About every four or five days, each of them could figure on losing several lambs to that bear. They all tried to trap or kill him but failed time after time. Herb Hamilton's sheepherder, Bernie, lost his horse, but after searching for a couple of hours, he finally found the horse and rode bareback toward camp. Suddenly he came around a bend in the trail, and there was "Mister Bear" eating on a freshly killed lamb.

This man brought the bear cub back to his cabin. *Yampa-Egeria Museum.*

Bernie said, "My horse, Old Brownie, wheeled and started to run away, but I leaned forward, grabbed him around the neck and said, 'Don't leave me now, Brownie!'" Both the horse and Bernie made it back to their camp in record time. Herb Hamilton thought it was the same bear that followed his herd out of Wheeler Basin down into Long Gulch, where they finally shot him.

> *Francis Moore had his sheep on the Greenridge pasture for the summer in the early 1950s. Irvin Thompson was the herder at the time. A bear was getting into the sheep each night and killing lambs; Irvin set the bear trap and caught a bear a few nights later. When he went to the trap the next morning, he carried his rifle with him so he could shoot the bear. When he got to the trap, he enjoyed watching the bear. It was a beautiful animal even if it was lunging and roaring as it tried to come toward Irvin. Irvin shot but did not kill the bear. The bear continued to lunge and roar at him. Irvin was shooting a lever-action Winchester rifle, and when he "threw in another shell," the gun jammed. Irvin said he was very calm, and he took the jammed shell out of the rifle and shot the bear again.* [Francis added, "He probably wasn't that calm or the gun wouldn't have jammed."] *All the while, the bear was still lunging and trying to get out of the trap. This time, Irvin killed the bear. When he finally went to take the bear out of the trap, the bear was only caught by three toes and while lunging in the trap he had torn off two of those toes. One little toe was all that still held that bear! Irvin said, after that, he shot the bear first and admired him after he was dead.* [119]

Herb Moore told this story about the first days of Yampa:

> *A bear from the Greenridge area entered Moffat Avenue from the east and leisurely ambled down the street. This occurred during the middle of the day. Many people saw him and went frantically rushing for their guns, but in their excitement those who could find guns could not find ammunition and those who found ammunition could not find their guns. Consequently, Mr. Bear leisurely traveled the full length of the street, went on west up the hill and out of sight. No one fired a single shot. This happened in a town that prided itself on its proficient and talented hunters.* [120]

An article in an August 1907 newspaper stated:

Emory Clark and Charley Brannon had quite an interesting experience with a bear last Friday. They had gone to hunt horses and were several miles above the Sterner Reservoir on Egeria Creek when they found a 4-year-old colt and a cow which appeared to have been killed by some wild animal. Closer examination revealed bear tracks and the men sat down to wait until bruin should appear, although neither was armed with a gun.

In about half an hour the bear was seen slowly emerging from the trees creeping toward the carcass of the cow. Clark mounted his horse and circled around, being within a short distance of the bear before he was noticed. The bear at once started toward the trees, but Clark roped him with his lasso and the faithful dog kept biting his heels until glad to escape he climbed a tree. Before reaching this place of refuge Clark roped the bear three times, but it was able to loosen the rope with its paws and extricate itself.

Mr. Brannon and the dog kept Mr. Bear treed until Clark rode four miles to Fred Able's after a gun. Several times the bear attempted to come down the tree, but each time was driven back by the dog. On returning, Mr. Clark shot the bear through the chest. The animal was found to be about 5 feet long and 3 feet high. It weighed about 250 pounds. [121]

Other animals were featured in the lives of the people who lived in the region. The following tale took place when H.E. Moore was living in his homestead cabin on what is now Routt County Road 17.

Albert Bird had found a young fawn whose mother was evidently killed. The fawn was starving, so Albert brought the young deer home and was able to feed it and keep it alive. It became used to people and was not a bit afraid of anyone. As it got older, it naturally roamed farther from Albert's house. When the little buck was a two-year-old, he had a good set of antlers. One day, very early in the morning, he went over to H.E. Moore's cabin (a little more than a quarter mile from Albert's house). The deer jumped up onto the porch and started using his antlers to butt the tubs and pans. The noise woke H.E. out of a sound sleep, and when he went to see what was making the terrible racket, the deer just stood there and looked back at him. This made H.E. mad, so he grabbed his gun and drew a good bead on one of the deer's antlers about three inches above his head. The bullet blew the antler to shreds; it looked a little like a broom turned up in the air. It was a hard-enough blow that it almost knocked the deer out. He started to walk around in little tiny circles, around and around. Each circle got just a little larger as the deer got over being stunned. Finally, the deer got his senses back and ran toward his home. H.E. said that he always wondered what Albert thought of the stub that the deer brought home. But he didn't ask Albert.

Chickens were a crucial part of daily life for the people in the Yampa Valley. Chickens were both a source of eggs and meat. Those first settlers could not run to the store every day to buy eggs for breakfast or for baking, so almost every family had chickens. They needed the eggs, but chicken dinner on a Sunday was a special treat.

Most of the early settlers in this area raised their chickens by letting their hens set on the eggs. This worked rather well with some hens; other hens did not raise very many chicks. Those hens would let two or three chicks hatch; then they would take the two or three chicks and leave the nest. The rest of the eggs would get cold, and the last chicks would not hatch.

Some of the first homesteaders also kept ducks and geese. These could be used for meat but also furnished feathers for their pillows and comforters.

A fellow by the name of George Huffman lived at a house east of the Yampa Cemetery where the cottonwoods are growing. He was one of the earlier ones to raise chickens with a "store-bought brooder." His brooder used a kerosene lantern as the source of heat. This worked to keep the chicks

Earle and Bertha Moore feeding the ducks and chickens, about 1900. *Herold family collection.*

warm, but it was a fire danger. At Huffman's house, a lantern was knocked over and started a fire on the back porch. It scorched the side of the house, but he was very lucky, as it did not start the whole house on fire.

Even after Yampa was thriving as a town, chickens were important to the farmers and ranchers. Many housewives kept more chickens than they actually needed for their own egg consumption. The extra eggs could then be traded to the grocery stores in town.

Pigs were another animal that most homesteaders raised. Families bought weaner pigs, then fed them for several months until they were big enough to butcher. Other ranchers kept a sow or two to raise litters of pigs for resale. There always seemed to be a local market for these animals.

From the time the first families came into Egeria until the mid-1950s, almost every ranch and homestead kept at least one milk cow. For a while, Yampa had a creamery that utilized the local milk and cream for butter. It was closed by about 1915. After the railroad came into the valley, many of the different homesteaders kept several animals and sold the cream or milk. At first, this went to a processor in Steamboat Springs. Later, the cream was shipped to Denver to be processed. The trains picked up the cream cans each day; the empty cans would be shipped back in a day or two.

Cows, like other animals, have their own individual personalities, some good—some bad. Francis Moore told about a difficult milk cow he had raised.[122] When the forest ranger that worked at the Eagle Rock station moved, he sold H.E. Moore a milk cow. It was a Holstein and had been bred to a "fancy" Guernsey bull from down in the Eagle area. The ranger told H.E. that if the cow had a heifer calf, it would be worth fifty dollars when it hit the ground. Francis said that it was a heifer calf, but it did not have the good qualities of the two breeds. It gave the amount of milk of the Guernsey and had the butterfat of the Holstein. (Just backward!) The old Holstein cow was a very good cow and was quite gentle. The young cow looked like a Guernsey and must have also gotten her disposition from the bull. She was much more cantankerous than her mother. Francis said that they were only milking four or five cows at that time. A hired hand, Fred Francis, was working for H.E. on the ranch and could milk any of the cows except that Guernsey. That young Guernsey cow would stand quietly for anyone to milk her except for Fred Francis. She just did not like him and would go out of her way to kick him.

This would not be complete without a dog story.

Charlie Sanders was a fellow who came from Arkansas. He was very proud of an old dog of his he called Dewey.[123] Charlie felt that Dewey was

Pigs on Congor Mesa, near McCoy, Colorado, circa 1920. *Hayne, Ray, Schrupp collection.*

a real good hunting dog because he had run and hunted raccoons before coming to Routt County. One day they were in a wagon on their way to clean a ditch and they saw a coyote on the top of a sagebrush ridge. Charlie told old Dewey "sic–sic," and Dewey immediately went up and over that ridge after the coyote. A few minutes later, Dewey reappeared, running back toward the wagon as fast as he could with two coyotes nipping at his heels. After that, Charlie could never get old Dewey to leave the wagon when they went on the ditch line.

Trying to rope bears were not the only wild animals on which young men practiced their lassoing abilities. Gordon Moffatt was riding into town with some of his buddies. They were all dressed up to impress the ladies at the dance that night. They rode past a skunk at a lope and they decided to rope that striped animal. Gordon made a good catch. As he jerked the rope tight, the skunk hit the end and flew up off the ground, then landed in the saddle with him. Needless to say, he didn't attend the dance that night, as he didn't think the girls would be impressed with that particular perfume.

Skunks have always liked to include chicken in their diet. One year, Gladys Moore had gotten one hundred day-old baby chicks. These young chicks always had to stay in the small end of the chicken house under the electric brooder. For two or three nights, a few chicks were killed and a few were missing. She blocked every window and hole so no predators could get into the room, or so she thought. The next night, Gladys was the only person home when she heard a ruckus from the chickens. She went to see; there was a pile of dead chicks in one corner and a skunk still in the room. She grabbed the .22 rifle and with one shot killed that skunk. Until that time, the family wasn't even aware that Gladys knew how to shoot.

Wild animals have always been of interest to the boys and girls of the valley, as related by Francis Moore:

> *My brother, Earle, said when he was a teenage boy, there was a pair of golden eagles with a nest high up on one of the Laughlin Buttes. He and a neighbor boy about Earle's same age, Wright Huffman, kept watching the eagles and noticed they were going and coming to the nest much more frequently, so they supposed there were little eaglets in the nest. The boys wondered how many and how big those little birds were, so they decided to climb up and find out. It was a hard, difficult climb; Wright was above Earle and had come to a place where there were only very small cracks and bumps to support him. Just like a bullet, a screaming eagle came out of nowhere. It even brushed Wright with a wing tip. If she had hit him any harder, she probably would have knocked him off the rock. The boys decided the secret, of how many and how big the baby birds were, was no longer important and quickly climbed down.* [124]

Birds were not the only creatures that intrigued the locals. People tried to gentle small animals, squirrels and badgers, as well as some of the larger animals, bear cubs, bobcat cubs and even mountain lion cubs.

Northwest Colorado was no different than any other place. Animals both large and small were important to the people in the area. Everyone seemed to have an animal they hated the most—or an animal they liked the best.

Unidentified man holding a mountain lion cub. *Herold family collection.*

5
CELEBRATIONS AND FESTIVITIES

Holidays were observed in Northwestern Colorado just as they were in other rural areas at that time. The funny and amusing times experienced during different events helped folks through the sad times. The support of family members and friends was truly important then, just as it is now. The following incidents are a random mix told by numerous people.

Different organizations formed during the late nineteenth and early twentieth centuries, both for socialization and for education. When the weather was agreeable, they might have outside activities; during the winter, they met indoors. Those organizations included but are not limited to the American Legion, the Masons, the Eastern Star, the Woodsmen of the World, the Ladies Aid Society, the Missionary Society, the Women's Union, a ski club, the Camp Fire Girls and 4-H clubs. At times, there were both Girl Scout and Boy Scout organizations. The Yampa Band included both adults and younger members.

NEW YEARS

The Tom Woods family lived in the house that George Huffman built on a four-acre tract of land that he purchased from Robert Laughlin, just south and a little east of the Yampa Cemetery. One year when the children, Robert (Bob) and Janet, were in high school, the Woods family invited several

Camp Fire Girls ready for their camping trip, 1927. *Herold family collection.*

guests to a "watch-night" party for New Year's Eve. [Probably in the 1920s.] *All went well until about two minutes to midnight; Bob grabbed the old twelve-gauge shotgun and went outside. Since there was snow on the ground, he stayed on the porch and just stuck the gun barrel past the eaves of the roof. When someone shouted "mid-night" Bob pulled the trigger. "Whoom"—He blew the electric line apart—this, of course, put the whole party in the dark.*[125]

One New Year's Eve, Mr. and Mrs. James Redmond entertained at their home on Hunt Creek with a six-course dinner at eight o'clock. This was followed by cards, and at midnight, a delicious repast was served, followed by a sculpturing match, where one of the guests displayed great talent by molding an elephant. Games and music lasted until eight o'clock in the morning, when breakfast was served. Those present were Frank Wright, Mr. and Mrs. Loren Bird, Bruce Roupe and family, Howard Allen and family, and Mrs. Mary Buckley.[126]

Ruth Cole mentions that in 1951, their son, his wife and their grandson had joined them for the day. They all had a "baked ham dinner and it was very good." After dinner, they had a "big canasta game" that ran late into the evening.[127]

Lila Allen stated that having a taffy pull was a big thing back then. "During holidays we would all gather at one of our houses and have a big meal and have a big time. We used to dance in each other's homes and play lots of card games."[128]

Frank Wright

Frank Wright driving his team and sled. *Yampa-Egeria Museum.*

WINTER

Sledding and ski parties were favorite winter pastimes for all ages. These events would evolve into supper parties then perhaps an evening of card games—canasta was a favorite.

During the 1920s, Yampa had a Winter Sports Club for both adults and children. There was at least one ski festival that included ski jumping, cross-country ski racing and street events. This was well attended by high school–age athletes as well as those out of school.

When she was in high school, Thelma (Margerum) Griest said that one of the best parties she ever had was having all her friends over to her house for a taffy pull (in 1928 or 1929).[129] Taffy pulls were held in the winter, as the early residents felt that in warm weather, taffy would not pop when it was pulled or would not fully set.

During the cold months, some of the different social organizations held parties and supper events. The Eastern Star and Masons often held a Cherry Pie Social to celebrate George Washington's birthday. The Ladies Aid Society and the Missionary Society held afternoon teas or luncheon parties for their members. By the 1950s, the Ladies Aid was holding an annual Ground Hog Day dinner. This let everyone socialize during the middle of winter when the weather was the worst.

Above: Laughlin family sledding party, about 1912. *Herold family collection.*

Right: Even the youngest children enjoyed sledding, about 1912. *Herold family collection.*

Skijoring on Moffat Avenue in Yampa during the Winter Carnival, 1927. *Herold family collection.*

During the First World War, many of those same organizations held events to raise money for the Red Cross. Baked goods and handworked items were favorite articles sold by the women's organizations. War bond campaigns were organized by the different towns; money was pledged, raised locally and sent to the county collection center. One of the projects for the schoolchildren was knitting items for the soldiers. Sweaters, socks and even washrags were knitted by both children and adults and given to the Red Cross to be sent overseas.

SUMMER

During the summer, the young people of the area got together for different types of entertainment. Dancing was a favorite pastime. The first settlers would hold a gathering in their homes. Lewis Wilson told of one such dance: "There was a dance at the Hoag place, about a mile and a half down the road from Yampa. The house was large enough to accommodate two dance sets." (The cabin was about twelve feet by fourteen feet in size. This didn't allow two square dance sets much room to "swing their partner.") As schoolhouses were built, they became common gathering places for holding dances.

A trip to Trappers Lake was a great family vacation, circa 1920. *Herold family collection.*

Each community had people who enjoyed playing instruments for a dance; harmonicas, violins and banjos were all popular. By the 1920s, some of the schoolhouses and homes had pianos. The town halls from State Bridge to Hayden could be rented. Many times the young men, and sometimes the young ladies, would ride twenty or thirty miles to attend the festivities.

Both young people and families made trips to Trappers Lake during the summer. A pack trip over the Flattops to spend several days fishing at the lake seemed to be a favorite vacation. These jaunts even made newsworthy events in the *Yampa Leader*: "A jolly party consisting of Sam Bird, Henry Page, Ben Laughlin, Robert Laughlin, Robert Gray, Charlie Crossan and Misses Lila Crossan, Carrie Smith, Edna Walker and Mrs. Samuelson as chaperon with pack horses and provisions left for Trappers Lake Monday for an outing."[130]

Trappers Lake was just one destination for summer camping trips. Whenever visitors from other areas came into the valley, camping, fishing or hunting anywhere in the Gore or Flattop regions was a place for summer excursions. This was an easy way to entertain and impress city relatives.

Rodeos, horse racing, bucking horses, foot races and baseball games were favorite forms of entertainment from the arrival of the earliest settlers to

The Royal Hotel is the backdrop for a group of riders leaving for a pack trip to the Flattops, circa 1915. *Yampa-Egeria Museum.*

A fishing trip was one way to entertain visitors, circa 1910. *Herold family collection.*

This rodeo was held in Yampa just north of the school. Notice the parked cars to form the arena, circa 1920. *Yampa-Egeria Museum.*

modern times. The Fourth of July was always a time for listening to speeches, getting together, meeting with neighbors (everyone in the valley from Burns to Brown's Park was a neighbor) and testing one's athletic abilities.

About 1910, the Yampa Brass Band was started with just a few individuals who played for their own enjoyment. It quickly evolved into a larger band that played and marched during special occasions.

> *At the 4th of July celebration in 1908, good speeches were made during the exercises at the grove by Rev. JR. Browne, Judge Charles A. Morning, County Treasurer Hamilton and Attorney W.B. McCleliand.*
>
> *The quarter mile dash, free-for-all, was won by Gray Dick, ridden by his owner, Luther Lee. Joe, a horse from the Dawson ranch at Hayden, ridden by Frank Arnold, took second place.*
>
> *The relay horse race, 2½ miles, five horses to each rider, who used the same saddle and transferred it to each new mount, was won by Bennie Laughlin of Yampa with Gray Dick and four other horses. One of Ed Watson's riders with a string of horses from the Lazy 7 outfit won second money.*
>
> *The ball game on the second day was won by Yampa, with a score of 8 to Steamboat's 7.*

The Yampa Brass Band was formed with both adults and high school students. *Yampa-Egeria Museum.*

The Yampa Band marched down Moffat Avenue in Yampa, circa 1910. *Yampa-Egeria Museum.*

"Ben Laughlin rode the winner." Horse races were held on the streets of all towns in the Valley. *Herold family collection.*

In the bucking contest the purse for the best rider was divided between Emory Clark and Spence, the judges calling it a tie. Fox, Hinckley's bay from Steamboat, was declared to be the worst horse.

One of the most enjoyable features of the celebration was the show given at the Town Hall Saturday night by the Wilcox Novelty Co. its moving pictures and illustrated songs delighting a large audience. Mr. Wilcox also furnished some splendid music for the dances at the hall Friday and Saturday nights. By a special request another show was given Sunday night, a large audience enjoying a complete change of bill.[131]

Pony express races were very popular; most celebrations seemed to include at least one. Sometimes, the horses would each have a saddle already in place, and the rider switched horses. At other times, the rider had to switch his saddle from one horse to the next. Each event set the distance for the race and the number of horses to be included, usually three, four or five. Each horse would run a quarter or a half mile.

The Stetson "boys," Jimmy and Glen, were riding in a pony express race in the 1950s. When changing the saddle from one horse to the next, Glen threw the saddle onto the next horse; he did not bother to tighten his cinch. He then vaulted into the saddle to continue the race. He pulled that cinch up tight after he and the horse were at a full run. Yes, they did win that race.

Bucking contests were held on Moffat Avenue in Yampa, as well as in various fields and arenas throughout the valley. *Yampa-Egeria Museum.*

Team pulling contest on Yampa's Main Street, John Schalnus, teamster, 1984. *Yampa-Egeria Museum, Fogg collection.*

Farmers and Ranchers would bring their best draft horses into town for "team pulls." These occurred during the 1920s and into the 1930s but were again enjoyed during the 1970s and 1980s.

Another favorite time to meet neighbors was the annual Pioneer Picnic. Each year, it was held in different towns throughout the valley. According to the *Steamboat Pilot*, the following events were part of the 1906 affair at Yampa:

> *The Pioneers had a successful gathering at Yampa. The town was overflowing with people on Wednesday and Thursday. Receptions held on Wednesday and Thursday evenings were both well attended. At dinner the guests were seated in the order in which they arrived in the county, earliest first. There were a number of speeches honoring Routt County pioneers of the past. Officers elected were: president, H.J. Hernage; vice president, F. E. Milner; treasurer, D.W. Whipple; secretary, C.H. Leckenby and historian, John A. Campbell.*
>
> *Hayden and Yampa played ball both days and took turns winning. Walter Laughlin won the calf roping, tying two calves in two minutes, 20 seconds. Walter Laughlin's saddle horse, ridden by Sammie Bird, won the saddle race. Another horse race, 100 yards, turn a stake, was tied by Bennie Laughlin and a man from Hayden. The young men's race was won*

Rodeos and picnics were a time to meet friends and enjoy a day off work. *Yampa-Egeria Museum.*

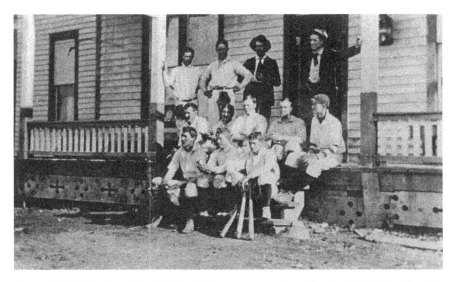

Yampa Ball Club, 1907. Identified in the bottom row are Sam Nay (*center*) Will Nay (*far right*). *Herold family collection.*

by Alfred Buck and the race for men over sixty was won by M. J. Rhoads. Then, Walter Laughlin won the race for men over 200 pounds.

Pinears, the famous bucking horse, threw Pollard, the champion White River rider one day and was ridden to a finish the next day by Roy Coberly of Middle Park.[132]

During the late 1920s and early 1930s, the flat open area on the hill west of Moffat Avenue in Yampa was used not only for rodeos, but also had a flat area that was used as a landing strip and as an airport. Thus, the name, "Airport Hill." Flying exhibitions were held at that location several different years. Many times, after a performance, a pilot would take locals for a ride in their plane. Most charged for a ride, the cost depended on the duration of the ride.[133]

An event reported in 1913:

The Hernage Mercantile Company had Rush Razee, world champion fancy shooter. Give an exhibition of shooting with the Remington guns at Yampa the first of the week that was well worth seeing. Mr. Razee

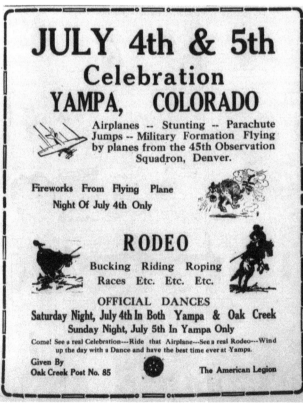

Above: "Lindy and Ann" standing in front of the airplane after their ride. Airport Hill west of Yampa in 1929. *Herold family collection.*

Left: Air shows as well as rodeos were held at Airport Hill just west of Moffat Avenue during the 1920s and early 1930s. *From the* Oak Creek Times-Yampa Leader, *July 2, 1931.*

used the latest style revolvers, rifles and shotguns. He shot small marbles thrown in the air with the rifle and broke as high as five targets thrown in the air at one time with the shotgun, picking them out one at a time and breaking all before they reached the ground. He threw two targets in the air shot one and turned around and shot the other without any apparent difficulty. Many other fancy shots were made to show the perfect working of the various guns.[134]

FALL

After the weather turned cool, the residents of the valley fished and hunted for their winters supply of meat. This activity was necessary but also enjoyable. Many people turned it into a vacation. Deer, elk, antelope and bear meat was all frozen for the winter. Fish could be salted and stored in barrels or dried for use during the winter. Even today, many residents consider wild game a good source of protein.

Meat was not the only item that the early residents used to combine both pleasure and necessity. Some families picnicked and camped while gathering berries for jams to store for the winter.

Women as well as men hunted deer and elk. Mildred and Marie Schrupp on Congor Mesa near McCoy. *Hayne-Ray-Schrupp collection.*

HALLOWEEN

By 1915, Halloween was a night for pranks and mischief for the younger men of the area. The acts were normally not dangerous or property destroying, just "monkeyshines" that gave the fellows something to do with their abundant energy.

The young kids enjoyed "tic-tacking" the windows of residents. This consisted of using an empty wooden spool that had notches cut into the sides. A string was wound around this and a pencil or other round stick used as a handle. When this was spun against the windows a very odd noise resounded. The mischief makers then ran away before the residents could identify them.

> One year three boys ran their "tic-tacks" down the front window of the Royal Hotel. Lem Lindsey had heard those noises before and was prepared. Lem jerked the door open and hollered "sic 'em." His dog ran out after the boys. Two of the kids ran around to the sides of the building, but Carey Trantham ran straight out into that wide Moffat Avenue with the dog yapping after him. Carey was quickly caught and identified. What happened after that remains a mystery.

For many years, the big school bell, which hung in the belfry of the old wood frame building in Yampa, would be robbed of its clapper on Halloween night.[135] This would ensure that the bell would not ring the following morning. (This is the same bell that is on display in front of the current elementary school.) A few days later, the clapper would be mailed to the principal of the school. A great prank, until one year the principal secured another clapper and the bell continued to ring without interruption. So that ended the fun for the kids.

Something that all the boys around the area did was get together each Halloween night to find what mischief they could do to the town people.[136]

One year during the week before Halloween, the teachers and other adults of town had been telling the kids that they were going to hire three marshals to patrol the town and stop any trouble that the kids were planning. That particular year, Melvin Burris and Francis Moore each rode into town from their separate homes. They met at the hitch rail in front of Kawin's General store and left their horses tied there. They then went on foot with some of the other kids their age.

During the evening, the kids went around the town, but they spent more time looking over their shoulders than doing much in the way of mischief. The group that Francis and Melvin were with decided to call it quits fairly early in the evening (probably 9:00 or 10:00 p.m.) They were at the north end of town by that time. Francis and Melvin walked back up to the hitch rail to get their horses and ride on to their homes.

When they got to the hitch rack in front of the store, they found all three of the officers that had been hired to stop the Halloween pranks. The officers were trying to pull a horse-drawn grader up onto the porch in front of the door to the store to block the door. Francis and Melvin joined in and helped move the grader, so the door could not be opened until the grader was moved.

Charley Arnold (one of the fellows hired as a town marshal) said that Harry Kawin, the owner of the store, would be disappointed if nothing was done to him at Halloween.

It was probably the year before that, when some of the boys (the fellows just out of high school) moved the outhouse that was behind the general store that Harry Kawin ran. They picked it up, carried it around the store, and carefully placed it in against the front door, so that the door could not be opened until the outhouse was moved.

When Kawin got to the store the next morning, he moved the outhouse just enough so he could get the door opened. Kawin (who retained some of his foreign accent) said, "Dat's all right, whoever it belongs to can come get it and take it home."

He then went into his store so he could open the store for the day; after that, he went back and opened the back door and exclaimed, emphatically, "Mein Got! It's mine!"

Of course, that was too good of a story for it to remain untold.[137]

Another year at Halloween, Aldus Klumker was delivering a load of coal from the mines at Oak Creek. It was somewhat after dusk when he got into town, and as he looked around, he found his brothers locked up in the town jail. (This jail is now on display on the west side of the museum in Yampa.) Aldus drove his truck up to the jail and hooked on to the bars at the window. He pulled the window out so the boys inside could climb outside.

Aldus took the truckload of coal on home and parked it to be unloaded the next day. He decided to go back into town and join in the fun. He got into town and looked for his brothers; when he finally found them, they were back in jail. He walked up and asked them, "Why are you still here? I pulled

Above: Yampa's historic jail, photo taken in 2003. *Herold family collection.*

Left: Thelma and Gladys Margerum dressed for a Halloween party, about 1915. *Herold family collection.*

the window out so you could leave." He no more than got the words out of his mouth when he felt a hand on his arm. The next thing he knew, he was in jail right along with his brothers.

The girls and young ladies did not seem to "tip over the outhouses" or pull other pranks; instead, they would get together at someone's house for a party. They played games, such as charades or hot potato. Often, they would end the evening with the boys joining them while they pulled a batch of taffy or held an impromptu dance.

BIRTHDAYS

No matter what time of year, a birthday has always been an excuse for a family reunion, a celebration dinner or a party. The following stories were found in the early newspapers.

Thirty-five friends had a surprise party for James H. Cole's nineteenth birthday. In 1914, they "took that young man so completely unawares as to their coming that they actually discovered him about to answer the telephone in abbreviated garments to respond to a fictitious call."[138] They danced until a late hour and had refreshments of cake, ice cream and punch. The partygoers left several nice gifts.

Frances Laughlin Kindly remembered: "The 1915 gathering of members of the Ladies' Aid and the Missionary societies yesterday at Mrs. Mark Cole's was one of the largest of the kind ever held at Yampa. It was given in honor of Mrs. Frances Laughlin on the occasion of her birthday. During the afternoon Mrs. Laughlin was presented with a handsome string of gold beads, the gift of the two societies. The presentation speech was

Picnics and birthday parties were often held in VanCamp's grove. *Left to right*: Maude Macfarlane, Frances Laughlin, Alice Laughlin, unidentified, Herb Moore and Ruth Cole. *Herold family collection.*

made by Mrs. John Cole in a most pleasing manner. Mrs. Laughlin was also the recipient of a number of other gifts from her numerous friends."[139]

"Mr. Jim Phillips was given a surprise party for his 21st birthday. About thirty guests enjoyed dancing the evening away. At 12 o'clock refreshments were served. The guests did not leave the Phillips home until the early hours of the morning."[140]

Summer birthdays seemed to be celebrated with a card party or a dance. Holding a taffy pull or ice cream party was a favorite way to celebrate a wintertime birthday. Ice cream was a wintertime treat, as snow or ice cut from the creeks or ponds could be used in their ice cream freezers.

THANKSGIVING

Even raised locally, turkeys were a popular item on the Thanksgiving table. On November 28, 1924, the *Yampa Leader* announced on the front page: "Turkeys for Thanksgiving. E.M. Stice of Toponas drove into Oak Creek Saturday with a load of turkeys and chickens. There were 65 turkeys; all fat birds and Mr. Stice had no difficulty in disposing of them at a good price."

Everyone in the area had a gun or rifle of some kind. One event that was enjoyed was a good shooting contest. Turkey shoots were often held; the winner did not receive an actual turkey, but a prize. Many a time, each person to shoot would pay fifty cents or a dollar into the "pot" and then the two or three best shots would split the pot. The best shot got the entire pot or at least the largest split of the top three placings.

The 1911 newspaper had this advertisement: "Turkey Shoot and Dance on Thanksgiving Day and evening, Thurs. Nov 30. Dance at Yampa Town Hall, music by Babcock Orchestra. Everybody invited. John L. Williams."[141]

CHRISTMAS

During the 1880s, Christmas and other holidays could sometimes be very hard for those first settlers. The isolation of the area in the winter made social occasions especially hard for the women and children, as they did not get outside to visit their neighbors as often as the men did.

Mary King wrote to the paper with the following story: "As Christmas season draws near it reminds us of our first and succeeding Christmas occasions in Egeria Park, more than 38 years ago. We had just come from

Breckenridge, Summit County, to make our home on King Creek [south of Toponas]."

Preston King went back to Breckenridge for winter supplies, then started home with his loaded wagon, trailing bobsleds behind. It snowed all the way down the Blue, and when he reached the Gore Range, the snow was so deep that he had to divide his load, making three trips across the range to Rock Creek and to the McDonald ranch house. It was difficult to make his way through several feet of snow, and he was thirteen days on the road. Thus, he spent his Christmas on the trail, not reaching home until the day before New Years.

"The wind had been blowing furiously all the time he was away and it found many places of entrance in our newly built log house, making it a hard matter to keep warm." The family did not attempt to celebrate Christmas but waited until New Years, since Mr. King had arrived home the day before. Mrs. King could only remember one thing they had to eat: "that was a roast of some kind, venison I suppose, just as I was taking it from the oven Billy Jacobs, from Sunnyside divide, came in and stayed with us for dinner. This was the first time he had ever been at our house, but later he and his family came to be very pleasant neighbors." She did not remember if any gifts were exchanged.

The next year, when friends from Breckenridge had come in and settled on their ranches, they had "sociable and happy times together." They each took one of the holidays and entertained the others.[142]

In 1902, Christmas services were held in the new Yampa church building even though the bell tower was not finished. "The building for the Congregational Church [now the Yampa Bible Church] was begun in the summer of 1902 and first used on Christmas day of the same year."[143]

The first settlers met for church services in private homes. That would lead us to believe that the Christmas services were held in private homes also. When the parishioners outgrew private homes, services were held in the Yampa Hall, currently known as the Masonic Hall.[144]

> *It was in 1915 when Fred Mohr received a hatchet for Christmas. He would have been eight or nine years old at the time.*
>
> *"I was so happy that I immediately went outside, climbed up on a pole fence and started singing 'Peter, Peter, Pumpkin Eater' while at the same time whacking the fence with my new hatchet. But alas! Once too often, and I hit my leg instead of the pole. I started yelling, threw my hatchet and headed for the house to show Mom. I still carry the scar where I chopped myself to the bone."*[145]

Fred also told about Christmas dinner in 1925. They had a large gobbler that weighed thirty-five pounds. He was not only big but also mean and even struck Emelia Mohr with his wings. They decided it was time to butcher him. He was so large that Mrs. Mohr had to cook him in the copper wash boiler.[146] All their friends and neighbors were invited for Christmas dinner. Travel was by sleigh, so the horses were put into the barn and fed for the night.

Mrs. Mohr was always an excellent cook; this time she set a "bountiful dinner." They then spent the afternoon playing games and visiting. Later that evening, they had another meal. No one wanted to travel at night, so everyone spent the night with the Mohrs and traveled home early the next morning in time to do the morning chores on their own places.

> *The house roof was leaking so Herb Moore hired Christian Mohr to put a "pitched roof" on the house.* [Until that time the roof would have had a rounded board crown with sod and dirt on the top.] *At the time, Francis Moore was 4 or 5 years old so it would have been 1913 or 1914. He had been given a toolbox with a set of tools for Christmas that year. Fred, Christian's son, accompanied his father part of the time. Both Francis and Fred used that Christmas set of tools to "help" build the roof.*[147]

Ruth and Mark Cole spent Christmas Eve 1950 with their eldest son (Walt) and his family.[148] They had a Christmas Eve supper, but they also celebrated their son's thirty-third birthday. After they ate, it was their family tradition to put up their Christmas tree and decorate it. Ruth does not tell us if her other son, Garth "Bub," was with them that Christmas.

There was not much money available to most of those early settlers, but the previous descriptions are representative stories about the different seasons and events of the year. These accounts demonstrate that everyone enjoyed visiting with family, friends and neighbors. People traveled to visit close neighbors and friends, but they also visited with friends from Brown's Park, Sunny Side, Burns Hole and beyond.

6

More Chronicles, Narratives
and Anecdotes

Major events in a nation create stories that are memorable and ones that are passed down from generation to generation. Routt County was not any worse or any better than other rural areas of the United States during Prohibition or the Great Depression years. Unpredictable weather was another reason for legends to be created. War has always created memorable incidents and created heroes at home and in actual battle. Accidents and illness brought their own tales, and the land itself often created a good story.

One of the most significant events to affect Northwestern Colorado was World War I . The war started in Europe in June 1914. The United States officially entered the war in April 1917. That Great War finally ended in November 1918. When the United States entered, many of the boys from Routt County joined up to fight "the war to end all wars." Until that time, the farthest that many of those young men had been away from home was the neighboring towns to ride in a rodeo or the like. That war had a major effect on those men and the families that stayed home and remained in the area.

According to the *Steamboat Pilot*, 716 people from Routt County joined one of the military services during those years.[149] It didn't seem to matter where each soldier went, boot camp was about the same for each man. Of those who served, 22 died in action in Europe. Some of those fellows were in the army, some in the navy and some in the marines.

World War I soldiers at the funeral procession for Willard Brown. Moffat Avenue in Yampa, Colorado, 1918. *Herold family collection.*

The following was related by a Routt County soldier, Julius Herold, who arrived in France just prior to November 11, 1918, when the armistice was signed:

> *We shipped out from Camp Dix in New Jersey about the first of October. We shipped on a small converted cattle boat about 250 feet long. We had to sleep in hammocks so close to one another that the next guy's feet were against your shoulder. They would all sway the way the boat swayed. And when they got out of time with one another the guys would do a little cussing. Well it took us eleven days to get across to England. They would go most of the day in one direction then at night they would turn sharply and go some distance in another direction to fool any subs that might be in the area. We landed in the fog at Liverpool, England....*
>
> *We were sent to Winchester; then one morning when we went to breakfast, we also got a couple sandwiches handed to us in a paper bag. We were told to load up in cars to be taken down to the docks at Southampton. We stood around there until about noontime. We cleaned up our sandwiches, thinking that was what they were for—our lunch. About 3:00 they started loading on a ship to take us across the English Channel. The first solder to board*

was placed in the corner, then next one in front of him with his pack against the other's belly, and that was the way it went till the end of the line. Then they started another line and that was the way it was all over the ship as far as one could see. They never gave us any order to unsling our equipment and after standing that way for as long as we could, we unslung our packs by unhooking the straps of the fellow in front of us letting the packs fall to the floor. After we could stand no longer, we laid down on top of our packs. One man's legs might have been under two other guys legs....We didn't unload at LaHavre [sic] until about 9:00 a.m. the next day. We marched in columns of four to a camp about six miles inland from the dock. There was no stopping for rest. One medical officer was struggling to make time to the head of the line, saying, "Don't them damn fools up there ahead have any sense to stop? There are men falling out all along the line!" Well, we got to camp and had orders to unsling our packs and stand by. We were apt to move out without being fed and it was already about noon. I guess the sandwiches they gave us the day before were meant to hold us over. We did stay there long enough to get a meal.[150]

Julius Herold was in the Army of Occupation at Coblenz until July 10, 1919. Quite often the supplies did not keep up with the soldiers. The German and French armies had both been in the area before the U.S. soldiers arrived, so there was not much food for either the local residents or the newly arriving soldiers. After they had been marching for several days, this was his story:

Now the cooks had saved a lot of bacon fat. They probably had a couple hundred pounds of the fat by then. Well, one of the officers had the bright idea of putting that grease on top of our helmets which we wore at that time. He thought they shined nice with the grease on them. We'd go down to the mess hall and get a cup full of grease for the squad. It wasn't long before we learned that a little grease could fetch a meal of raw potato pancakes and coffee. By then we were found out and we couldn't get any more grease.[151]

The residents in the Yampa Valley supported the American troops in many ways.[152] Each community had its own groups. The following is one example:

The Yampa branch of the Red Cross was started in December 1917. The officers were all local women with 180 members in the first drive. They had auctions, donations, "chicken" funds and other events; they

The Oak Creek Chapter Red Cross workers. *Left to right, back row*: Mrs. Jones, Mrs. Richerdson, Mrs. Higgins and Mable Stephens; *front*: Alice Biggs, Mrs. Bird and a French nurse, 1918. *Herold family collection.*

raised $2,243 as their contribution to the county chapter. Both the Red Cross workers and the Junior Red Cross workers collected clothing, knitted items and rolled bandages. In school, the first and second grade students knitted washcloths. (One fellow said that he was sure they all had to be washed before they were sent on, as little boys' grubby fingers did not knit well.) The older students and adults knitted and sewed sweaters, socks and other items. They turned in more than eight hundred items to the district chapter to be sent "over there."

The liberty bond drives were separate from the Red Cross. Each town or small settlement had its own drives, and the money from those collections was turned over to the banks to be sent to the central distributing office. There were several different drives, with the Yampa area residents contributing more than $30,000. Of the three liberty bond drives, the third was the largest; the total contributions from Routt County were $199,250.

FRANCIS MOORE RELATED SOME of changes that the Depression era brought to Yampa. "Because of the Great Depression, as it has been called, there were many adjustments in and around Yampa."[153] It started in 1929, but its effects lasted much longer, especially in this area.

Many small banks across the nation were forced to close. The Bank of Yampa was included. The Colorado State Banking Commission sent Bob Hubbard as receiver for the Yampa Bank, with full authority to sell all assets of the bank for cash, but cash was one thing people did not have. Evidently, there were no restrictions on Hubbard; he had the authority to set the price on all items, regardless of their true value. As a result, he sold some mighty cheap real estate in and around Yampa; he bought some of it himself. The bank had a mortgage on the Burris Ranch, which was about one mile east of Eagle Rock. That was one of the first places Hubbard both sold and bought; this included Burris's car. That meant that Hubbard was no longer afoot. Although Hubbard probably did not violate any actual laws, deals like that did not make Hubbard very popular in the Yampa area for many years. The biggest problem was that no one had cash to spare.

The Burris family took what few personal belongings they had left and went back to Oklahoma. Mr. Burris told Francis Moore, "The first year we grew head lettuce on the place, the crop was very good and the price excellent. I could have paid off the loan completely that year, but I paid only half the loan and bought a new car, thinking we could easily pay the remainder next year. But we never had another crop as good and the price was less than half of the amount that it was that first year. So, we lost everything."

The Bank of Yampa was forced to close when the stock market crashed. The Yampa Ladies Aid then used the building for the town library. Photo taken about 1980. *Herold family collection.*

Hubbard priced three other ranches, the Choate, the Powell and the Scribner, at $1,000 each. Francis didn't remember who bought the Choate place (south of Phippsburg). Pat Martindale bought the Powell place. Again, Hubbard bought a place for himself, the Scribner ranch. (This was about eight miles west of Yampa.) A person with a few thousand dollars in cash could have owned an amazing amount of land. In four or five years, the value of those places increased at least ten times.

After selling all assets of the Bank of Yampa at extremely low prices and paying all the debts of the bank, each depositor of the bank was finally paid about 25 percent of what he had on deposit at the time of closure. Hubbard then bought Andy Black's ranch (on the Yampa River about six miles north of Phippsburg). He married Betty Alfred and started raising sheep. Much of that ranch, as well as some others, is now under the water of Stagecoach Reservoir.

> *Arnold Powell was a large land and cattle owner, as well as the president of the Bank of Yampa. When it went bankrupt, Powell was one of the largest stockholders in the bank; the bank foreclosure completely broke him. The Powell family soon left the area, went to California and were forced to live very sparingly for the rest of their lives.*
>
> *Arnold Powell and his wife came to the United States from England. They all had a heavy English accent. Both Arnold and their daughter, Nettie, soon lost their English accent, but Mrs. Powell never did. When they were leaving this area, Mrs. Powell came to bid the Moore family good-by. She gave Francis a fancy little cup and saucer, saying, "Take good care of it, it is 'impotted' (meaning imported)."*[154]

During the Depression, the WPA (Work Projects Administration, in effect from 1935 to 1943, to relieve the national unemployment) did different types of public service projects. WPA crews performed work in small towns such as Yampa, but they also built rock bridges, roads in the forest and highway projects over some of the mountain passes.

The original water mains for the town of Yampa were wooden pipes completed in 1910.[155] Those pipes were built of wooden slats and held together by metal wire banding. During the Depression, the WPA came to Yampa and worked on the old pipes to change them to metal. The men all dug the ditches by hand. There were thirty or so in the group; at times, there may have been as many as fifty. They all lived in tents set up where the Forest Service buildings are now. To keep the tents warm during the winter,

Yampa's first water mains were laid down Main Street in 1909. *Yampa-Egeria Museum.*

one man went around keeping the fires lit in the stoves during the day, and another did this during the night.

The town of Yampa is built on round river rocks. Those rocks were found under a scant two to six inches of topsoil. When they dug the ditches for the water mains, there was a lot of those river rocks piled up around the edges of the ditches. They ran the rocks through a crusher and covered the street with two and a half to three inches of that crushed rock. Several side streets were also graveled at that time. After those streets were graveled, some of the people grumbled about the rocks on the streets—the women could not walk across the street easily in their high-heeled shoes. It took a year or more for the crushed rock to pack down and make a "decent" street.

When the ditches for those pipes were open, John Hughes went "out on the town" one night. (At the time, he was living at the old Severs (Bemis) house on the west edge of town.)[156] He drank and played cards, but when he tried to go back to his house, he fell into an open ditch and started hollering. He screamed "loud enough to wake up the whole town." In fact, "He screamed loud enough that everyone thought there must be a murder going on." Someone got him out of the ditch and he finally went toward his home.

At about the same time, there was a CCC (the Civilian Conservation Corps stayed in effect nationally from 1933 to 1942) camp set up just inside

In 1934, a Civilian Conservation Corp (CCC) camp was set up about eight miles southwest of Yampa on the Bear River. *Courtesy of the Yampa, U. S. Forest Service.*

the Forest Service boundary up the Bear River Road toward Stillwater.[157] The people in the CCC were younger men than those in the WPA. Benson Male was the youth minister at the Yampa Congregational Church at the time. He took a group of ten or fifteen young people up to the CCC camp to entertain the boys there. The group of boys from the church (including Francis Moore) sang some songs, and Benson gave a talk. There were some young African Americans included in the group working at the camp. After Benson gave his sermon, one of the young fellows told Benson that they had a group of four that did a little singing, so Benson invited them to come and sing at the church. They did. Francis said that they were very good: "They had <u>real</u> harmony." He figured that they probably laughed to themselves about the singing attempts of the local church group. Francis added that the African Americans at the CCC camp were only there for a very short time. They were quickly moved to another location; Francis did not speculate on the reason for their move.

CHARLIE SANDERS WAS AN "Arkansawyer" who was here during Prohibition and the Depression. During that time, he made his own alcohol. Pink Easterly told the following story:

Charlie Sanders and Ralph Maddox were drinking "chalk" (this is what they called the first run of boot-leg liquor) at Charlie's place. They looked up and saw Oren Gray riding down the road toward Charlie's house; Oren was the revenuer at the time. Charlie and Ralph took off for the willows, down by the creek, and left Charlie's wife, Nan, with the crock of whiskey. That didn't bother Nan a bit, she was in the process of making bread; she just smeared some flour on the outside of the crock and threw a towel over the top of it. She then went on with the making of her bread. Oren Gray came in and looked through the house. He could smell the boot-leg whiskey, but he didn't find it.[158]

Joe Johnson bought Ben Laughlin's homestead. This was located about one mile northeast of the junction of Highway 131 and County Road 21A. Joe also had another place with a house northwest of Ben Laughlin's place. Joe evidently operated stills for bootleg whiskey at both of those places. Joe had not finished paying Ben Laughlin for the land in 1924, so as a final payment, he gave Bennie one of his two Cadillac cars. Bennie said that Joe must have just barely kept ahead of the revenuers (revenue agents) because when Bennie greased that old car, he found several bullet holes in the bottom. Bennie speculated that someone had shot at Joe when he was going quite fast over a hill.

By the time World War II came, Routt County had changed. Because of the ease of transportation, many of the residents had traveled farther from the area. Also, some of their fathers or uncles had been to France or Germany in the First World War. Still, many of the young people from this area served in the armed forces, the army, the navy and the newly formed air force. One change from World War I was that the personnel were stationed in both Europe and the Pacific.

Another difference was women were now serving their country in the various services. They were not allowed in the combat zones but were still vital in the supporting roles. Ruby Ray joined the Women's Army Corps in 1943. She had graduated from high school in Yampa and owned and operated a beauty salon in Steamboat Springs before joining the army. In the service, she served as a mail clerk, a filing clerk and a typist. She was honorably discharged in 1945 with the rank of sergeant.

The earliest settlers in this area found the winters very unpredictable. The following illustrates some of that, both the normal problems associated with winter and some not so common: "The first school board meeting was held May 1, 1883 at the (Henry) Crawford's. [Henry Crawford was a brother to

Above: Lawrence Davis was a member of the band on the president's ship at the beginning of World War II. *Herold family collection.*

Right: Ruby Ray joined the Women's Army Corps in 1943. *Hayne-Ray collection.*

James Crawford of Steamboat Springs.] All the board members came on skis and the snow was so deep that they were able to ski over the top of most of the fences."[159]

Francis Moore thought the winter the Laughlin family had to take their stock up to Lawson Creek for early spring feed was the same year that his mother, Bertha Laughlin Moore, recalled the school board meeting being held the first day of May.[160] The meeting was to be held at the school just south of the Yampa Cemetery, and all those who came from the Yampa area and beyond skied right over the top of the fences on their way down the valley.

> *Frank Blue was a person that had a problem with his speech. When he was in a hurry, or excited he stuttered. He told of being in the Little Flattops up above Crosho Lake one winter on skis, he came out of that steep hill just north of Crosho and looked down on that frozen lake and decided the nearest way home was straight across the lake. He said, "I cut loose and went flying down the hill and out on the lake. But there was no ice under the snow; just snow lying on the water! Maybe you think I didn't sk-sk-ski then!"*[161]

"The stage running between Yampa and Hot Sulfur Springs made its last trip for the season Wednesday. [This was the first week in November 1905.] Jim Edmonson took the coach to Steamboat for the winter. He reports the snow a foot deep on the Gore Range. Jim intends to go back to Grand County, to work for the railroad, in the Gore Canyon."[162]

Herb and Bertha Moore told of one very unusual year.[163] It was 1895, the year of their marriage. Robert Laughlin was off prospecting for gold at Cripple Creek as he often was. Bertha wanted her father, Robert, to give her away in marriage. It was arranged for the wedding to be at an uncle's place, a few miles from Colorado Springs, on January 20. Herb and Bertha went all the way with a team and buggy with very little snow on either pass (Berthoud Pass and Gore Pass). With the wedding over, they started back for Yampa. They stopped overnight at a stage stop just west of Denver. The next morning, it was snowing so hard they waited. It snowed and snowed, wet heavy snow, about thirty inches deep. Two days later, with the weather clearing, Herb decided to move on. They didn't have enough money to continue to stay there. Also, he reasoned, with the team, he might find work around Georgetown or Empire, as there was a considerable amount of mining going on in that area. But the farther they went toward the mountains, the less snow they found. So, they just kept on going, right over the top of Berthoud Pass with just a little more snow than when they went to Colorado Springs. The farther they traveled, the less the snow. Finally, they trotted down the street in Yampa with dust rising from under the horses' feet. It was one of the first days of February.

After a hard winter, the spring runoff could be almost as bad as the winter. In 1913, the following announcement was included in the *Steamboat Pilot*: "Ice jams are causing trouble in the Yampa River. High water is causing damage throughout Egeria Park. The Watson Creek Bridge near the Herb Moore place was washed out."[164]

In the early 1920s, another spring runoff caused problems on Moffat Avenue in Yampa. A photo of that shows water entirely across the street. What damage did the water cause to the basements and first floors in the houses?

The following stories show that summers also had unpredictable weather:

When Carey Trantham and Francis Moore were fairly young, John Cole had the "Do Drop Place" (John had either bought the homestead from William Bird or else he leased it from the Birds). John had planted the fields to lettuce. Carey, Francis and two other boys were caught in the rain while they were helping weed the lettuce. They went into the barn to get out of the weather. It started hailing, large hailstones, about the size of marbles. Carey Trantham reached out of the door, to pick up a hailstone that was larger yet, about the size of a quarter. Just then, a bolt of lightning struck. The lightning didn't touch any of the other boys, just Carey. He had leaned over to reach the hailstone, and evidently having three points on the ground made him a better conductor for the lightning bolt. He got quite a jolt. It burned him everyplace that the metal buttons of his bib overalls touched him.[165]

"B.F. Allen was in town today for the first time since his mix-up with a streak of lightening."[166] While driving in the cows at his ranch on Watson creek, Allen was knocked off his horse into a rock pile, his left shoulder was skinned up and one ear badly cut. When Allen picked himself up, his horse galloped away, but mud on the animal's knees indicated that it was also knocked down by the lightening.

Francis Moore ran the old separator (threshing machine) probably in the fall 1930.[167] He said that it was the prettiest October that he could remember; the weather was cool at night and warm during the day. On the first day of

Spring flood on Moffat Avenue in Yampa in the early 1920s. *Yampa-Egeria Museum.*

October, he started from the home ranch and threshed in different fields, working his way toward the Flattops and the Egeria Creek area. He finished up in Upper Egeria at Ote Perry's place on October 31. Francis said that everyone remarked how wonderful the weather had been. Earl Crowner Sr. told Francis that he would probably never see one as nice as that had been. (In 2005, Francis reminisced, "So far that has held true.") The night they finished, the weather changed, and it snowed three or four inches. The weather was warm enough the next day that Francis was able to pull the separator home with the old cat tractor.

Egeria Park was a lonesome land for those first settlers into the area. It has been called isolated and remote. Miners drifted into the mountains from both Denver and Colorado Springs in the 1870s. The roads and trails that those early miners used were rudimentary at best.

Because of the sparse population and the tricky access into the area, the lack of doctors was a major problem when the people arrived in Routt County during the 1880s. Those people in our valley were concerned about the same problems that we have today. Then they worried about typhoid, pneumonia and influenza; now we worry about West Nile, hantavirus and swine flu. Of course, accidents have always been a part of rural life. Probably the biggest difference is the amount of time it takes a victim to find good medical help.

Dave Gray told of the following incident:

> In 1884 James Scott brought his wife and two children to his Iron Spring
> Ranch. About March in 1885 Mrs. Scott became very ill. As there was
> no doctor in the settlement there was nothing to do but take her to a doctor
> on the other side of the range. She was placed on a trail sled which was
> drawn by six men on skis. The men were Sam Tharp, Herod Fulton,
> Louis Garbarino, Billy Whipple, Billy St. John and Frank Bird. Billy
> St. John was not a resident but spent much time in Egeria. Mrs. Scott
> was taken through Egeria Park, over Gore pass to Hot Sulphur Springs.
> From there she went by stage to Georgetown, a trip from which she did
> not return. [168]

> The Stafford family homesteaded the place just north of the Laughlin
> Buttes. They had two children, both girls. An epidemic of measles (one
> account said scarlet fever) had gone through the children of the valley. It
> did not affect the Laughlin children very much, they were sick, but back up
> and running around very soon. However, both the Stafford girls died. The
> parents had buried them on the sagebrush slope behind their house before
> any of the other homesteaders even knew they were ill. Because of their
> loss, the Staffords grew discouraged and lost interest in their place; they
> soon moved elsewhere. Bertha Laughlin always felt bad about the girls who
> had been her playmates, as she felt that she and the other Laughlin children
> might have passed the sickness on. [169]

Some of the doctors in the Yampa area had their practice in their homes, but the Monte Cristo Hotel and the Royal Hotel were also used as a hospital at various times. Dr. Cole had at least two rooms in his home that he used for hospital patients. He had a small cabin just outside his house where a couple nurses could stay. The nurses also cooked the meals for the patients.

The South Routt County doctors included Dr. Cole, Dr. Scholte, Dr. Male, Dr. Gilbert and Dr. Kennedy, but I am sure there were others. After transportation became faster and easier, people found doctors of their liking in Oak Creek or Steamboat Springs or Kremmling.

In 1905, the *Yampa Leader* reported the following in the local news section: "Miss Lila Crossan is quite sick with typhoid fever."[170]

Top: Dr. Cole had a small cabin behind his house where one or two nurses lived and cooked for the patients. *Herold family collection.*

Bottom: The south side of Moffat Avenue showing the Grand Hotel (The Monte Cristo Hotel) on the right. The Antler's Hotel is at center. *Yampa-Egeria Museum.*

"Mrs. Arthur Leighton was taken sick this week with typhoid fever. She is now at the Monte Cristo Hospital, where she is improving."

"Guy Jones had a serious accident last week. His team ran away breaking the tongue out of the hay rake and throwing him under the rake in front of the teeth, where he was rolled, tossed and bruised until the horses broke loose from the rig. When he was taken out it was found that one leg was broken, his head injured and other parts of his body bruised. We are glad to report that he is slowly improving."[171]

"Peter Lapham, who lives seven miles south of Yampa, is visiting in the valley this week. Mr. Lapham, known as 'Broncho Pete,' is suffering with a game leg, the result of a recent mix-up with a runaway horse."[172]

One of the saddest accidents that has ever happened in this vicinity resulted in the death of our friend and fellow townsman, J. W. Nichols, last Tuesday evening [1905]. Tuesday afternoon he, in company with P.A. Hughes, started for Mr. Hughes' ranch about three miles south of town, after a load of hay and when returning and making the turn just south of Michael Cox's ranch one of the wagon wheels dropped into a hole, which caused the load to upset. Mr. Hughes being in front and driving was pulled off the load and was not hurt, but Mr. Nichols, being near the center of the load, was struck by the rack and killed as the load rolled over him; the rack and load having left the running gears of the wagon. He was brought to town and it was found that his neck had been broken and that he had received a severe blow behind the right ear. The body was embalmed and is being held until relatives arrive, when he will be buried in the Yampa cemetery.[173]

Fred Ball, a man of German descent about 55 years of age was found dead beside the road near Toponas by Lee Combs, who was on his way in from Florence. Mr. Ball was a prospector and owned some property near Pueblo. Sunday evening after he had settled all his bills, he was talking with a friend here and said that he had not been feeling well for a few days, that his heart seemed to bother him, and he believed he would go over to Hot Sulphur. As he could not stand the heat, he got up early and started on foot, and when found had apparently been sitting on a rock to rest, when he was stricken with heart failure. He was found a few minutes after his death and brought to town. An inquest and autopsy were held and it was found that his death was caused by heart failure. Undertaker W.H. Bashor, of Steamboat came up and took charge of the body which was laid to rest in the Yampa cemetery Tuesday.[174]

The following stories were told by Francis Moore:

My Dad (Herb Moore) said shortly after the Powells arrived in the area, their only daughter, Nettie, got real sick. Of course, at that time there were no telephones, and the nearest doctor was in Steamboat Springs. Arnold asked Dad to ride one of his fastest horses for the doctor. Dad said, "I guess I rode that poor horse to death, because I left him in the livery stable overnight and the next morning, he was dead."

Later, Arnold told Dad, "Don't feel guilty; the horse was not acting right before the trip and I probably should have sent a different horse."

The good news for both the Powells and Dad was that Nettie soon recovered from her sickness. Naturally, the Powells were very proud of Nettie. Mrs. Powell bragged, "Nettie speaks four languages correctly."[175]

Francis Moore got his threshing machine from a fellow by the name of Holly.[176] Holly had two sons, Floyd and Ed. The older son, Ed, was running the machine for Holly the first year Holly bought it. They were threshing for Bob Laughlin when the feeder of the machine jammed; too many bundles had been thrown onto it. Ed Holly was impatient and gave a big jerk on one of the chains. This was a short chain that went around two or three cogs. The machine started working again at that moment and wound Ed's hand into the cogs. The people around got him out of the machine and to the doctor, but blood poisoning set in and he soon died. Holly did finish the grain at Bob Laughlin's place, but when he went to Herb Moore's place (the next place in line for threshing), he told Herb that he just couldn't stand to be around the machine. Whenever he looked at the machine, he would think of Ed.

Holly then offered to sell the thresher to Herb. Herb and Francis decided to go ahead and buy it. They finished threshing for all the people whom Holly had promised to put up grain.

Francis ran that separator (the local people called the threshing machine a separator) for about ten years; his was about the only machine in this end of the county when he started. He covered not only the immediate area around Yampa but also went as far as Pinnacle to the west, just over the divide at Red Dirt to the south, Perry's to the east, Kaiser's and Kissinger's on Egeria Creek and to the north as far as Middle Creek west of Oak Creek.

Jerry Reams homesteaded and built the buildings on what is called the Pink Easterly place on Greenridge.[177] Jerry's adopted son, Carl LaBounti, had just newly married Maude Height, and they filed on what we call the Dick Greenwood place. The year the influenza epidemic was so bad nationwide (1918–19), Carl was working for Herb Moore at the sawmill. Both he and Maude came down with the flu at the same time. Herb got real worried about them being so far from a doctor, so he moved them down to his ranch home, where Dr. Male could attend them on his regular rounds. Herb left a young fellow he had just hired to stay and keep the fire and tend to Carl and Maude since they were both flat in bed and real sick. Herb returned to the mill and didn't go back to the ranch until the weekend. He found the caretaker had been gone for two days. The house was freezing cold, and Carl was delirious with fever. Carl died two or three days later. For the rest of his life, Herb felt guilt whenever he thought of Carl's death because he had left the care and needs of those two in the hands of an inexperienced, irresponsible young man who proved to be a quitter. The good news was that Maude survived her bout with the flu. Several years later, she married Evert Wilson.

A side note to this story is that Dr. Male was proud that out of all the patients he had in the area around Yampa and Toponas, Carl was the only death. Most other doctors lost a far greater percentage of patients during that terribly severe outbreak of flu at the close of World War I. Most of the deaths were caused by dehydration or pneumonia. Dr. Male treated his patients for that instead of treating for the flu.

Dr. Male had a right to be proud of the lives he saved during that influenza epidemic; the following shows the losses that happened elsewhere in Colorado.

The influenza epidemic reached Colorado during 1918 and 1919. "The mountainous areas were especially hard hit. Silverton's population was 1,150; when they were hit by the flu, 833 people died; this was nearly 75% of the town's population. In ten months the flu had claimed the lives of 7,783 Coloradoans."[178]

The following notice was in the *Steamboat Pilot*: "All Schools Day—May 7 is cancelled. The program for all-schools day in Steamboat Springs, Saturday, May 7, will not take place as announced because of an epidemic of measles and chicken-pox among the children."

Not all accidents had an unfortunate ending. The following story was told like this:

Two brothers had gone south of Yampa and put a large load of hay onto their wagon. They stopped in town on their way back to their house on upper Watson Creek and picked up the latest newspaper. One brother was driving the team; the other brother was sitting on top of the load reading the news while riding in comfort. Something happened, perhaps the wagon hit a badger hole or maybe something on the wagon broke, but the wagon turned over spilling the load of hay. The driver could not see his brother, so assumed that he was hurt and buried under the load. He frantically and hurriedly pawed at the hay hoping to reach his brother before he suffocated. After a time, he looked around the load far enough to see the back of the spilled hay. His brother was reclining on the spilled hay and was continuing to leisurely read the newspaper.

When we think of change in the valley, we tend to think of the changes caused by human beings: buildings, ditches, plowed fields and so on. These are certainly not the only changes that have occurred during the last 150 years or so. Nature has a way of weathering and altering our surroundings. Landmarks that we think are permanent aren't necessarily so. Francis Moore mentioned the following change that occurred to Sand Point. The sandstone that he refers to is a type of volcanic ash.

When I was growing up each time one looked at the Flattop Mountains west of Yampa, we always saw a large sandstone peak just on the north end of those mountains. That peak was known as Sand Point. To show as large as it did from this distance it must have been two hundred fifty feet in height, and it was quite white as the sandstone in this area always is. So, we had Dome Peak on the South end of the Flattops and Sand Point on the north end. It was a well-known landmark of the area. Then about 1934, Sand Point just disappeared. Everyone batted their eyes and it was still gone. Finally, someone got curious enough to go see where it went, the report was "it's there all right; it's scattered down that steep rocky slope for about a half mile. It's among all those other slide rocks." Evidently the base gave away and the majority of that point just went tumbling.[179]

Another landmark that has changed dramatically during the last 150 years is the rock formation at the front of the Devil's Grave mesa. This large mesa is located northwest of Yampa and can be seen from County Road 17.

H.E. Moore said that when he first came into the area, the "tombstone" (natural rock column) at the front of the Devil's Grave was much taller than the grave (the mesa area to the north-west of the tombstone). There was also very little distance between the tombstone monument and the rocks behind it. One could just see a hint of daylight between them. Of course, when one looks at it today, erosion over time has had an effect on the rock. There is considerable distance between the two, and the tombstone portion is lower than the mesa.

There is an old postcard that had a photograph titled "Balancing Rock, near Yampa, Colorado." This rock is found on the eastern side of Wheeler

Above: Pictured here in 2006, the Devil's Grave is located northwest of Yampa. The "tombstone" has eroded over tthe last 150 years. *Herold family collection.*

Left: A postcard from 1921 shows the Balancing Rock near Yampa. *Yampa-Egeria Museum.*

Basin and was still there in 1999. It is on private property and not as large and prominent as some of the other volcanic rocks in the area; it has not remained in the public eye. Perhaps it, too, will erode, fall and no longer be a landmark.

TIME CONTINUES TO MARCH on. Everything changes, the people, the structures and even the land. It just seems to change at a slower pace in Northwestern Colorado.

NOTES

Chapter 1

1. Godfrey, "First Egeria Park Settlers," section 4, 1; T. Laughlin, oral communication, 1955.
2. Moore, "Some Things I Have Been Told." These and Moore's other unpublished manuscripts are in the author's collection.
3. Ibid.
4. F. Moore, oral communication, 2004.
5. Moore, interview, July 1, 2004.
6. Sparkman, "Look Back."
7. Moore, "Some Things I Have Been Told."
8. Ibid.
9. Hughel, *Chew Bunch*, 47–48.
10. Ibid., 99.
11. Steele, interview.
12. *Yampa Leader*, July 1, 1905, 4.
13. Gray, *Recollections of an Egeria Park Pioneer*.
14. *Yampa Leader*, January 6, 1905, 4.
15. "Passed Bad Checks," *Yampa Leader*, August 19, 1905, 4.
16. Moore, interview, July 2004.

Chapter 2

17. Nay, *There Was Always a Sam*, 31.
18. Ibid., 32.
19. Nay, letter, Monday 8th (196?). Date unreadable on letter in author's collection.
20. Nay, *There Was Always a Sam*, 35.
21. Moore, interview, June 9, 1999.
22. Ibid.
23. Ibid.
24. Ibid.
25. *Steamboat Pilot*, July 7, 1933.
26. Herold, letter, September 10, 1910.
27. Ibid.; Herold, "Autobiography"; J. Herold, oral communication. The autobiography is in the author's collection
28. C. Herold, oral communication, September 1965.
29. *Routt County Sentinel*, July 22, 1921.
30. *Steamboat Pilot*, December 9, 1927.
31. Moore, "Some Things I Have Been Told."
32. B. Laughlin, oral communication.
33. G. Moore, oral communication.
34. Montgomery, "Story of a Colorado Pioneer."
35. Moore, interview, September 20, 2005.
36. Nay, *There Was Always a Sam*, 3.
37. Wren, *Steamboat Pilot*, August 1955.

Chapter 3

38. Moore, interview, September 20, 2005.
39. Moore, interview, August 30, 2004.
40. Moore interview, February 2, 2006.
41. Moore, interview, July 1, 2005.
42. *Yampa Leader*, July 29, 1905, 1.
43. *Yampa Leader*, August 5, 1905, 4.
44. "Grand Family," *Yampa Leader*, December 19, 1913.
45. Moore, interview, June 19, 2003.
46. Morning, "Early Experiences at Yampa."
47. H. Moore, oral communication, 1955.

48. "Yampa, South Routt Community Is 100 Years Young," *Steamboat Pilot,* April 15, 1976, 2A.
49. Gray, *Recollections,* 6.
50. Pritchett, *Maggie By My Side,* 1, 7, 31.
51. Crossan, "Life of a Pioneer." This unpublished manuscript can be found in the Yampa-Egeria Museum.
52. Moore, interview, August 26, 2005.
53. Pritchett, *Maggie By My Side,* 1, 7, 31.
54. Moore, interview, February 2, 2006.
55. "Yampa, South Routt Community Is 100 Years Young."
56. Moore, interview, August 26, 2005.
57. Herold, "Autobiography."
58. Moore, interview, December 5, 2005.
59. Moore, interview, September 20, 2005.
60. Moore, interview, August 26, 2005.
61. Moore, "Some Things I Have Been Told."
62. Moore, interview, July 1, 2004.
63. *Yampa Leader,* December 23, 1910.
64. *Steamboat Pilot,* May 19, 1955.
65. Moore, "Some Things I Have Been Told."
66. Moore, interview, September 20, 2005.
67. Moore, "Some Answers."
68. C. Herold, oral communication, August 1963.
69. *Steamboat Pilot,* April 23, 1953.
70. *Steamboat Pilot,* November 30, 1939.
71. Mohr, "Autobiography."
72. Montgomery, "Story of a Colorado Pioneer."
73. *Yampa Leader,* July 8, 1905, 1.
74. Moore, "Some Things I Have Been Told."
75. Moore, interview, August 30, 2004.
76. Ibid.
77. Wren, "Lucky Cuss!"
78. Moore, interview, June 19, 2003.
79. Perry, "Memories." This manuscript may be found in the collection of the Yampa-Egeria Museum.
80. Moore, interview, February 2, 2006.
81. Redmond, "Allen Basin Reservoir Co."
82. Ibid.
83. Moore, interview, July 1, 2004.

84. Ibid.
85. Squire, "Taming the Mean Ones."
86. Moore, interview, September 20, 2005.
87. Moore, interview, June 25, 2008.
88. Long, oral communication.
89. Moore, interview, September 20, 2005.
90. *Yampa Leader*, April 24, 1914, 1.
91. *Yampa Leader*, April 10, 1914, 1.
92. *Yampa Leader*, August 5, 1905, 4.
93. Gray, *Recollections*, 5.
94. Ibid.
95. Whipple, "More Early History."
96. Moore, interview, September 20, 2005.

Chapter 4

97. Moore, "A Few Incidents from My Memory.".
98. Ibid.
99. "Local and Personal," *Routt County Republican*. July 28, 1916, 8.
100. Moore, "Few More Thoughts of Days Gone By."
101. Moore, interview, June 19, 2003.
102. Moore, "Some Things I Have Been Told."
103. Conner, interview.
104. Ibid.
105. Zeman, *Three Wire Winter*, Spring 1976.
106. Long, oral communication.
107. Moore, "Few More Thoughts of Days Gone By."
108. *Yampa Leader*, March 4, 1910, 8.
109. Moore, "More Memories of Days Gone By."
110. Squire, "Taming the Mean Ones," 205.
111. Ibid.
112. T. Laughlin, oral communication.
113. Ibid.
114. Moore, interview, June 19, 2003.
115. Pritchett, *Maggie By My Side*, 21.
116. "Big Bear Hunt in Routt County—Bears Killing Stock," *Yampa Leader*, April 16, 1909, 4.
117. Moore, "Few More Thoughts of Days Gone By."

118. Ibid.
119. Moore, interview, August 30, 2004.
120. Moore, "Some Things I Have Been Told."
121. *Yampa Leader*, August 1907.
122. Moore, interview, June 19, 2003.
123. Moore, interview, August 30, 2004.
124. Moore, "Some Things I Have Been Told."

Chapter 5

125. Moore, "Few More Thoughts of Days Gone By."
126. *Yampa Leader*, January 5, 1923, 1.
127. Cole, personal diary.
128. Mack and Eck, "Lila From Egeria Park," 15.
129. Griest, oral communication.
130. *Yampa Leader*, July 8, 1905, 4.
131. "Echoes of the Fourth," *Yampa Leader*, July 11, 1908.
132. *Steamboat Pilot*, June 27, 1906, 1.
133. Moore, "Few More Thoughts of Days Gone By."
134. "Fancy Shooting," *Yampa Leader*, June 27, 1913, 1.
135. Moore, "Few Comical Incidents From My Memory."
136. Moore, interview, June 12, 1993.
137. Moore, "Few More Thoughts of Days Gone By."
138. *Yampa Leader*, May 8, 1914, 1.
139. *Yampa Leader*, August 6, 1915, 1.
140. *Yampa Leader*, July 17, 1914, 1.
141. "Turkey Shoot and Dance," *Yampa Leader*, November 17, 1911, 4.
142. King, "Christmas of the Early Days," *Steamboat Pilot*, July 27, 1934, 6.
143. "Church History," *Steamboat Pilot*, April 8, 1971, 7.
144. Mauch, *Yampa Bible Church*.
145. Mohr, "Autobiography." This autobiography may be found in the collection of the Yampa-Egeria Museum.
146. Ibid.
147. Moore, June 12, 1993.
148. Cole, personal diary.

Chapter 6

149. Honor Roll, Routt County, 1917, 1918, 1919, *Steamboat Pilot*, 1919.

150. Herold, "Autobiography."

151. Ibid.

152. Honor Roll, Routt County, 1917, 1918, 1919, *Steamboat Pilot*, 1919.

153. Moore, "Few More Thoughts of Days Gone By."

154. Moore, "Some Things I Have Been Told."

155. Moore, interview, May 31, 2004.

156. Ibid.

157. Ibid.

158. Moore, interview, June 9, 1999.

159. "Yampa, South Routt Community Is One Hundred Years Young," *Steamboat Pilot*, April 15, 1976, 2A.

160. Moore, "Few More Thoughts of Days Gone By."

161. Ibid.

162. *Yampa Leader*, November 4, 1905, 1.

163. Moore, "Some Things I Have Been Told."

164. *Steamboat Pilot*, April 2, 1913, 5.

165. Moore, interview, June 20, 2005.

166. *Yampa Leader*, June 4, 1909.

167. Moore, interview, September 20, 2005.

168. Gray, *Recollections*.

169. Moore, interview, June 9, 1999.

170. *Yampa Leader*, October 21, 1905.

171. *Yampa Leader*, August 29, 1905, 4.

172. Ibid.

173. *Yampa Leader*, September 30, 1905, 1.

174. *Yampa Leader*, September 2, 1904, 4.

175. Moore, "Some Things I Have Been Told."

176. Moore, interview, February 6, 2005.

177. Moore, "Few More Thoughts of Days Gone By."

178. Krudwig, *Hiking Through Colorado History*, 71.

179. Moore, "Few More Thoughts of Days Gone By."

BIBLIOGRAPHY

Cole, Ruth Laughlin. Personal Diary, 1950–1951.

Conner, Cecil. Interview, May 15, 2000.

Crossan, George C. "The Life of a Pioneer George Crooke Crossan." Unpublished manuscript, 2000.

Godfrey, Mrs. E.H. "First Egeria Park Settlers Encountered Hardships." *Steamboat Pilot,* July 27, 1934.

Gray, David S. *Recollections of an Egeria Park Pioneer.* Steamboat Springs, CO: Steamboat Pilot, 1941.

Griest, Thelma. Oral communication, June 1952.

Herold, Carl, Sr. Oral communication, August 1963.

———. Oral communication, September 1965.

Herold, Emma (Schmitt). Letter. September 10, 1910.

Herold, Julius. "Autobiography." Undated. Edited by Herold Nuwer, 1986.

———. Oral communication, 1964.

Honor Roll, Routt County, 1917, 1918, 1919. *Steamboat Pilot,* 1919.

Hughel, Avvon Chew. *The Chew Bunch in Brown's Park.* San Francisco: Scrimshaw Press, 1970.

King, Mrs. Preston. "A Christmas of the Early Days." *Steamboat Pilot,* July 27, 1934.

Krudwig, Vickie Leigh. *Hiking Through Colorado History.* Englewood, CO: Westcliffe Publishing, 1998.

Laughlin, Ben. Oral communication. 1953.

Laughlin, Tom. Oral communication. 1954–55.

Long, Linda. Oral communication. September 2019.

Look, Alfred A. *Bits of Colorado History*. Denver, CO: Golden Bell Press, 1977.

Mack, Letha, and Tanna Eck. "Lila From Egeria Park." *Three Wire Winter*, Spring 1976.

Mauch, Elizabeth A., ed. *Yampa Bible Church, 100 Years of Memories, 1902–2002*. N.p.: self-published, 2002.

Mohr, Fred. "Autobiography of Fred Henry Christian Mohr." Undated.

Montgomery, Ilda. "The Story of a Colorado Pioneer." *Yampa Leader*, November 28, 1924.

Moore, Francis. "A Few Comical Incidents from My Memory." 2001.

———. "A Few Incidents from My Memory." 2001.

———. "A Few More Thoughts of Days Gone By." 2002.

———. Interviews by author, 1993–2008.

———. "More Memories of Days Gone By." 2002.

———. Oral communication, 2004.

———. "Some Answers." 2002.

———. "Some Things I Have Been Told." 2001.

Moore, Gladys (Margarum). Oral communication, 1959.

Moore, H.E. Oral communication, 1955.

Morning, Charles A. "Early Experiences at Yampa and Hahns Peak." *Steamboat Pilot*, July 27, 1934.

Nay, Josephine. Letter, Monday 8th (196?).

Nay, Samuel, Jr. *There Was Always a Sam*. Garden Grove, CA: Keepsake Publishing, 2004.

Perry, Mae. "Memories." Unpublished manuscript 1979–1980.

Pritchett, Lulita Crawford. *Maggie By My Side*. 2nd ed. Parshall, CO: Grand County Historical Association, 1983.

Redmond, Wanda. "Allen Basin Reservoir Co, Inc." *CNCC History and Legends*, Spring 2005.

Routt County Republican. "Local and Personal." July 28, 1916.

Routt County Sentinel. July 22, 1921.

Sparkman, Shannan. "A Look Back—The Legacy of Tracy & Lant." Museum of Northwest Colorado. www.museumnwco.org/lookbackarticle.

Squire, Rube. "Taming the Mean Ones." *Colorado Magazine*, July 1962.

Steamboat Pilot. "All Schools Day—May 7 Is Cancelled." May 5, 1938.

———. April 2, 1913.

———. April 23, 1953.

———. "Church History." April 8, 1971.

———. December 9, 1927.

————. July 7, 1933.

————. November 30, 1939.

————. "Yampa Is One Town That Grew Up Naturally." July 30, 1964.

————. "Yampa, South Routt Community Is 100 Years Young." April 15, 1976.

Steele, Rene Chew. Interview, October 14, 2019.

Westerner Magazine, September 1947.

Whipple, Billy. "More Early History of Egeria Park." *Steamboat Pilot*, September 14, 1941.

Wren, Jean. "The Lucky Cuss! The Life and Times of a Cowboy Preacher." *Steamboat Magazine*, 1994.

Yampa Leader. April 10, 1914.

————. April 24, 1914.

————. August 5, 1905.

————. August 29, 1905.

————. "Big Bear Hunt in Routt County—Bears Killing Stock." April 16, 1909.

————. "Echoes of the Fourth" July 11, 1908.

————. December 23, 1910.

————. "Fancy Shooting." June 27, 1913.

————. "A Grand Family." December 19, 1913.

————. January 5, 1923.

————. January 6, 1905.

————. July 1, 1905.

————. July 8, 1905.

————. July 29, 1905.

————. June 4, 1909.

————. March 4, 1910.

————. November 4, 1905.

————. October 21, 1905.

————. "Passed Bad Checks." August 19, 1905.

————. September 2, 1904.

————. September 30, 1905.

————. "Turkey Shoot and Dance." November 17, 1911.

Zeman, Holly. *Three Wire Winter*, Spring 1976.

INDEX

About the Author

Rita Herold is a descendant of early settlers and pioneers of Routt County. She and her family live on and operate a fifth-generation centennial ranch near Yampa, Colorado. As she grew up listening to the stories of the area told by her father, grandfathers and great-uncles, her passion for history developed at an early age.

Rita graduated from Utah State University with a bachelor's degree in education. She taught grades kindergarten through twelfth and worked as an adjunct history teacher for both Colorado Northwestern Community College and Colorado Mountain College. Rita has given numerous talks and lectures for the Tread of Pioneers Museum, Tracks and Trails Museum and the Yampa–Egeria Museum. She has developed history tours of southern Routt County and history curriculums for students.

With community in mind, Rita has served as a longtime 4-H leader and Routt County Fair volunteer. She has been a board member and volunteer in the Cattle Women's Association, Routt County Preservation Board and the Yampa–Egeria Historical Society.

Rita enjoys writing, art, photography, traveling and her family. This is her second book.